CW01213599

ADVANCE PRAISE

"I have known Nick for about ten years and find him to be one of the brightest, most insightful, energetic, and dynamic leaders I have ever met. Writing The Passionate Workforce is a natural extension of his personality and desire to give back by helping others. The book's focus and Nick's assessment tool are so timely in today's workplace environment. As a former CEO and business owner, I understand the advantages and benefits of knowing your employees' passion quotient. Employing the strategies described in this book works, and you and your company will be the benefactors of that knowledge. This is a must-read."

—Tony Muraco, former President & CEO of Universal Window and Door LLC

"In the decade plus that I have known Nick, he has always strived for a high-performing culture at his company. Nick gets it. Culture matters. High performers matter, and having the right people matters. Nick has always been passionate about moving his companies and life along to greatness."

—Dan Mahr, President of Aalanco Service Corporation

"I have known Nick for nearly fifteen years, and during that time, I have been incredibly impressed by his ability to grow a business, grow his people, and grow his friendships—all at the same time. Nick has a gift for storytelling that captivates readers and leaves them wanting more. His writing is both eloquent and accessible, making it appealing to a wide range of audiences. In addition, he has a strong understanding of business, character development, and pacing, which allows him to craft compelling stories that stay with readers long after they've finished reading."

—MATT GARRETT, EXECUTIVE CHAIRMAN OF TGG ACCOUNTING

"I have known Nick since we met at a CEO peer group fifteen years ago. Nick was passionate then, and it's no surprise he has translated his passionate approach to his business to creating that same passion in his team. As a constant learner and observer of what is going on around him, Nick has distilled these concepts into a readable and usable form."

—ERIK DODIER, CO-FOUNDER & CEO OF RAFTERONE

"Nick Capman is an exceptional blend of business tactician and thoughtful leader. In my personal experience, I have found him to be a masterful communicator as well as a careful and deliberate listener. Able to rapidly identify the core issue at the heart of any discussion, Nick's breadth of knowledge in both business and leadership empower him to excel in developing solutions for positive outcomes. Now, in his book The Passionate Workforce, those unique strengths and insights are made accessible to all. Through them, I genuinely believe Nick has unlocked a new way of thinking about how we build our teams and how we look at structuring our companies. More so, he has generously provided each of us with our very own copies of that key."

—DAN BARKER, CEO OF WIKIMOTIVE

"I highly recommend *The Passionate Workforce*, written by Nicholas Capman, to anyone interested in developing their leadership skills. As a CEO with years of experience, Nick provides valuable insights and practical strategies for leading teams and building a 'human-centered' organization.

Nick's unique perspective on leadership is both insightful and practical. Whether you're a seasoned leader or just starting your career, *The Passionate Workforce* is full of actionable advice you can use to improve your leadership abilities."

—BOB YARD, PRESIDENT OF MERCURY WIRE PRODUCTS

"As a longtime entrepreneur and CEO, Nicholas Capman has captured the essence of creating a workforce that is passionate about their work. I have had the privilege of knowing Nicholas as a peer for several years and value his insight as a leader and executive. His Passionate Workforce Assessment guides you in identifying opportunities to bring your team's productivity to the next level. The 15 Pillars help you identify actions that you can take to ignite the passion in your team. The best part is that this is all measurable; you can see these strategies working. *The Passionate Workforce* is a must-have for any leader's library."

—DONNA DOROZINSKY, PRESIDENT & CEO OF JUST IN TIME GCP

"Nick brings the experience and wisdom of an entrepreneur who has built a thriving business from the ground up. Employee passion is so critical to success, but as a business owner myself, it's a puzzle I've struggled to solve my entire career. Finally, with this book, we have a coherent framework for establishing passion within an organization. Thank you, Nick!"

—DAVID MARLIN, PRESIDENT OF METACOMET SYSTEMS

"Inspired by a professor while earning his master's degree in business administration, Nicholas Capman had the vision and the passion to start his own business at a very young age. His drive, focus, determination, and solid leadership skills have inspired him to share strategies and tactics crucial to the development of a passionate workforce.

It is passion that motivates an individual to be successful at work and to live a life with purpose and meaning. Capman, President & CEO of the FDA Group LLC, takes on the role of leader and author in his book, The Passionate Workforce. In this book, Capman defines the 15 Pillars that are essential to encouraging and developing the passion of an individual who has the desire and drive to pursue excellence, to feel proud of the work they do while working at a job they truly enjoy, in an environment where the importance of a work/life balance is recognized and supported.

Individuals who are passionate about their job are more inclined to work hard on self-improvement, increasing their chances of success.

It is passion that motivates an individual to be successful at work and to live a life with purpose and meaning. It is that passion that Capman hopes to instill in others in his book, The Passionate Workforce."

—KARL MOISAN, PRESIDENT & CEO OF
HOMEFIELD CREDIT UNION

"In his book, The Passionate Workforce, Nicholas Capman not only reinforces the importance of passionate engagement as a basic core value for team members of a successful organization, but he also provides a roadmap for evaluating, instilling, and raising the passion of those team members. If you believe that people are the most valuable asset of an organization, this very readable book will provide you with an actionable way to enhance the culture, performance, and success of your company."

—James Rouse, Chair of Vistage Worldwide and former CEO of Arrhythmia Research Technology Inc.

"Insightful and compelling, The Passionate Workforce draws on author Nicholas Capman's immense experience and success as a business owner and CEO. He recognizes that individuals who love their jobs tend to be peak performers, drive quality outcomes, and promote an increasingly positive work environment, and he asks how can leaders directly influence, further accelerate, and incite passion in those who work for them. Mr. Capman's powerful exploration of this concept informs and guides his readers, providing proven strategies, tangible tools, and a formulaic approach to increasing workplace engagement and, in turn, a designed solution for generating more fulfilling and productive human-centered organizations."

—Tameryn Campbell, President & CEO of Masonic Health System of MA, Inc.

"Nick always provides a no-nonsense and thoughtful approach to business issues and resolution. As a fellow Vistage member, I have been fortunate enough to learn from Nick's insights and share his excitement for The Passionate Workforce! Use Nick's 15 Pillars within your business and relationships—the results will follow!"

—Brendan Hester, CEO of ePay Business Solutions, Inc

THE PASSIONATE WORKFORCE

THE
PASSIONATE
WORKFORCE

HOW TO CREATE AND MAINTAIN

MAXIMUM EMPLOYEE

ENGAGEMENT

NICHOLAS CAPMAN

LIONCREST
PUBLISHING

COPYRIGHT © 2024 NICHOLAS CAPMAN
All rights reserved.

THE PASSIONATE WORKFORCE
How to Create and Maintain Maximum Employee Engagement

FIRST EDITION

ISBN 978-1-5445-4448-9 *Hardcover*
      978-1-5445-4447-2 *Paperback*
      978-1-5445-4446-5 *Ebook*
      978-1-5445-4545-5 *Audiobook*

To my father, who has joined the Lord Almighty in Heaven—thank you for being a real-life superhero and for showing me that true fulfillment is found in dedicating your life to your wife and children.

CONTENTS

INTRODUCTION 15

1. WHY BEING PASSIONATE ABOUT YOUR WORKFORCE MATTERS ...21

2. THE PASSIONATE WORKFORCE SPECTRUM 31

3. PRIMING YOUR NEW HIRES FOR LONG-TERM PASSION 41

4. HOW TO KEEP YOUR WORKFORCE PASSIONATE 53

5. THE 15 PILLARS OF A PASSIONATE WORKFORCE 73

6. WHAT TYPE OF LEADER/MANAGER ARE YOU? 113

CONCLUSION 121

ACKNOWLEDGMENTS 123

ABOUT THE AUTHOR 125

INTRODUCTION

"You can't make people listen to you. You can't make them execute. That might be a temporary solution for a simple task. But to implement real change, to drive people to accomplish something truly complex or difficult or dangerous—you can't make people do those things. You have to lead them."
—JOCKO WILLINK, AUTHOR

Are you passionate about your job? Are your employees?

When I was in high school, I worked a few jobs through a temp agency, including one in a warehouse where I was required, at times, to operate a forklift. There was just one other guy, whom we'll call Rob, and our boss, whom we'll call Mr. Dube.

Mr. Dube always seemed like he was in a rush, like he didn't have time to give us any direction or even a thought. He simply told us to stack items on pallets, and then he went on his merry way. So, Rob and I, two high schoolers with no supervision, put our noses to the grindstone and got working.

Yeah, right.

It took all of five minutes before Rob asked if I wanted to race the forklifts.

(On an unrelated note, did you know forklifts can go as fast as ten miles per hour?)

Later, I would learn that the repercussions of wasting my time were more painful than just working in the first place, but at that naive age, all I knew was that if Rob wasn't going to work, then I wasn't going to either. It didn't help that Mr. Dube didn't give us his contact information, nor that the temp agency wasn't involved after making the assignment.

For a couple weeks, Rob and I clocked in, raced forklifts, hung out at the picnic table, raced again, then clocked out—until finally Mr. Dube came back to check on our progress. "You guys haven't done anything," he commented, looking bewildered.

Rob and I looked at each other. "Nope," we confirmed.

"Alright. Well, you can leave."

Looking back, I see that I didn't feel motivated because I was resentful. The person responsible for providing us with instructions should've also provided us with the leadership and management to execute the job well. He should've stoked our passion. However, there were no incentives, no enthusiasm, nothing that we could latch onto that would give us a sense of purpose.

This is why passion matters.

WHY PASSION MATTERS

A worker's performance is intrinsically impacted by whether they love or hate their job. It doesn't matter whether they're a banker, janitor, football player, or physicist—every worker falls somewhere along the Passionate Workforce Spectrum, where one end is passion and the other is resentment.

When a worker loves their job, they do everything they can to make sure their company succeeds. They arrive on time, help their colleagues, and are positive about the trajectory of the organization, both internally and in their conversations outside of work. They are creative, helpful, and passionate about achieving quality results, which translates into productive benefits for the entire workplace.

When a worker hates their job, they do the bare minimum, just enough so that they don't get fired. Instead of taking initiative, they ask, "What do you want me to do?" They show up late, demonstrate destructive behaviors, badmouth the company, and are clearly apathetic about the quality of their work. They become the subject of conversation during executive management meetings. Allowed to remain, their resentment spreads like cancer.

As a leader and manager, you likely ask yourself, *Am I getting the full value out of my workforce?* You're probably afraid that, as much as you train, guide, and oversee your employees, they will take advantage of you and the company. However, you may not realize that it's up to *you* to influence the right behavior in them.

In general, it's easy to identify the people on the far ends of the Passionate Workforce Spectrum. I'm sure you know who your A-players are and who is fully checked out. Recognizing the people in the middle, however, requires more analysis.

So, how do you know whether your employees are benefiting your company? How do you know whether they are passionate enough to produce high-quality work? You can ask them if they like their job a million different ways, but how can you know if they're giving you an honest answer? After all, you can't read their minds.

Blindly guessing at what your employees truly feel will likely leave you feeling stressed—and stumped. Luckily, there are 15 Pillars you can implement to ensure that every one of your employees feels passionate about their work. Before we discuss them, though, I want to share a bit about who I am.

WHO I AM

At twenty-three years old, I headed North American Business Development for a multinational pharmaceutical engineering firm. Then, in 2007, I founded my own company, The FDA Group, an eight-figure organization that helps pharmaceutical and medical device companies with FDA regulations. Since 2014, I've also been a member of Vistage, the world's largest CEO coaching and peer advisory organization for small and midsize business leaders. We meet once a month to listen to presentations from subject matter experts across a variety of business disciplines and to collaborate among ourselves to solve each others' business problems.

In addition, I'm a lifelong learner. Whether earning my MBA, reading business books, or hearing business leaders speak, I block out time every quarter to keep up with leadership and management theory. This long-standing practice has allowed me to acquire a large body of knowledge, notice consistent pieces of advice, and test and validate them in the real world—separating nice-sounding ideas from what actually works. For example, I've implemented EOS (Entrepreneurial Operating System) at my company as a way to improve the efficiency and efficacy of our operations.

Over time, a number of people have remarked that my approach is unique, that they like the way I think. I'm not an all-knowing magician, but through experience and curiosity, I've been able to crystallize what I've learned into an actionable system. Now I want to pay it forward and help you, just like my mentors helped me.

WHAT YOU'LL LEARN

In the following chapters, I will introduce you to different metrics you can use to validate my claim that passion equals higher performance. I would never ask you to blindly trust me, so you will learn how to implement measurables that concretely prove these strategies work. You will also learn how to prime your new hires for passion and maintain passion in your current employees.

In addition, I'll introduce you to the 15 Pillars that are the foundation of a passionate workforce. I'll explain the necessity of each and guide you through how to implement them so that your employees are fully engaged and executing to the best of their ability. Along the way, I think you'll find yourself becoming a more effective leader.

This book is meant for CEOs and executive teams who are looking for key nuggets of wisdom to level up their organizations, but over 90 percent of the information here can be used by any leader or manager. As long as someone reports to you, you can use this book to cultivate passion in your workforce. The information in this book also applies across industries.

It's important to note that I'm not here to transform your whole business. This book will not save a company that's in total decay; it's less like Gino Wickman's *Traction* and more like Jim Collins's *Good to Great*. But if you're looking to help your business reach its full potential, I will build on existing business theories with cutting-edge thoughts and present-day context.

Once you create a passionate workforce, you'll find that your company becomes human-centered. Suddenly, no one will be a cog in a wheel—including you. Instead of running around putting out fires all day, you'll feel bliss. You'll reclaim your time.

If you're ready to reduce your stress, improve your quality of life, and improve the lives of everyone who works for you, keep on reading.

CHAPTER 1

WHY BEING PASSIONATE ABOUT YOUR WORKFORCE MATTERS

"The journey of a thousand miles begins with a single step."
—Lao Tzu

Do you remember Mr. Dube, the manager who gave me no supervision or support when I operated a forklift? Later, I'll explain how decisions like his stack up against the 15 Pillars, but first, I want to assert that I could've been passionate about that job. In fact, any job—yes, *any*—can stoke passion.

Don't believe me? Let's start with an apples-to-apples comparison.

There's a story about a janitor who worked in JFK's administration who became renowned for saying, "I'm helping fly a man to the moon." It was true: he worked at NASA and if those scientists worked in a dirty place, they would have lower morale. They wouldn't perform as well.

The janitor was passionate about his work because he saw the connection between caring for the physical space and everyone operating with greater efficiency.

Likewise, I worked at Dunkin' Donuts as a porter for a time, and I *loved* that job. Water always accumulated in the backroom behind the blending machine, and the problem was hard to address, but my boss was respectfully candid about how to resolve it and why it was important to do so. Armed with constructive feedback, positive rapport, and a sense of purpose, I felt passionate about making everything spick-and-span.

However, it's not enough to know that any worker *can* be passionate about their job. You have to care that they *are*.

LEARN TO CARE

I didn't care about my employees in the early days of my business. As the CEO, I steered the ship, and all that mattered to me was that we were sailing smoothly. The other people on the journey with me didn't cross my mind.

Looking back, it's clear I was lower on Maslow's hierarchy; I wasn't anywhere near the level of self-actualization or even esteem. I was twenty-six years old, and my brain had just finished fully developing.

MASLOW'S HIERARCHY OF NEEDS

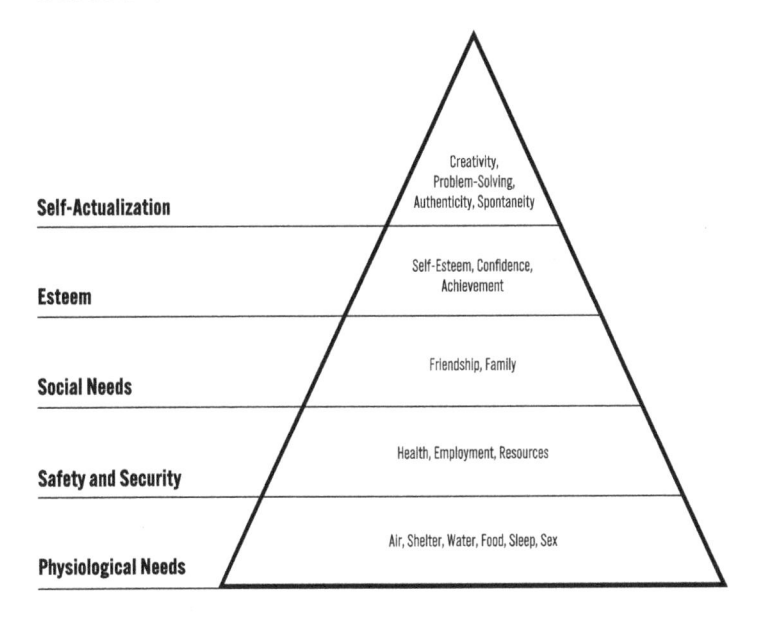

Self-Actualization	Creativity, Problem-Solving, Authenticity, Spontaneity
Esteem	Self-Esteem, Confidence, Achievement
Social Needs	Friendship, Family
Safety and Security	Health, Employment, Resources
Physiological Needs	Air, Shelter, Water, Food, Sleep, Sex

I'd never had any intention of running a multimillion-dollar organization—I just wanted to make some extra cash. When there was too much work for me to do it all on my own, I hired people, but I saw them as a means of getting what I wanted. I didn't understand that we should've had a mutually beneficial and supportive relationship.

Over time, I realized my approach wasn't going to work for two main reasons. First, we're all human. There's no good justification for treating someone like they're an emotionless tool made for profit. I began to feel bad knowing I was ignoring the fact that my team was made up of people who had their own history, family, and goals.

I didn't want to become Mr. Dube, unaware of how my lack of leadership and management would lead to my employees goofing off and resenting their job.

Second, as I matured and educated myself, I came to understand that not everything is about me. My desires were no longer the most important things in my life.

I often say happiness doesn't bring gratitude; gratitude brings happiness. Some people are depressed precisely because they only think about themselves: *I'm not getting paid enough. I'm working too many hours. People don't call me enough. I don't have what other people have.* If those people put their time and energy into making other people's lives better and forgot about their own lives for a while, they would actually increase their level of happiness.

You can only make truly effective decisions as a leader once you acknowledge your workforce's humanity and prioritize their needs over your own desires. Once you do, they will feel a greater sense of purpose, make greater contributions that expand the business and the bottom line.

For example, as I grew into my leadership role, I started setting reminders to recognize an employee every Friday. This is something I still do. However, if no one does anything special, I don't force it. It's essential to be sincere—fabricating recognition only shoots you in the foot. If you recognize people for doing the bare minimum, like showing up on time, people will wonder what is wrong with you or whether your expectations are really aligned with excellence.

Originally, I recognized people to pretend that I cared, because research says recognition from leadership is important. However, something interesting started to happen. Eventually, I *actually* began to care. I became someone who talks to Ann about candles, to Marty about interesting facts on the internet, and to Cory about the people who piss us off.

That evolution often happens when you make a change. If you don't know how to play soccer but commit to practicing every Friday, eventually you will learn. If you're an atheist but go to church every Sunday, you might very well end up believing in God. Fake it till you make it, right?

The more I genuinely cared and expressed that caring, the more I noticed my employees becoming visibly happier and more invested in their work. They expressed their gratitude for my gestures. When my birthday came around, they even bought me a really nice golf shirt and golf balls to show that they appreciated me, whereas they'd never bought me presents before.

Once I started getting really good at creating passion in people, I achieved what I call *The Patriot Discount*. After Tom Brady and the Patriots won one or two Super Bowls, players began accepting less money so that they could be part of the magic. By leading the team to victory, Bill Belichick was able to attract players and keep them there, because the probability of winning a Super Bowl with his leadership was higher than with any other coach or team.

As my executive management team and I leveled up, we saw that people who love what they do rarely have incentive to quit. Our turnover dropped, and the few employees who did leave called us a couple months later and—I kid you not—told us how much they regretted it. In some cases, we took them back; in other cases, we didn't. Now that we'd built a passionate team and were benefitting from the Patriot Discount, we could choose what was best for the organization.

In a way, you could argue it's selfish of me to care about my employees, because if I care about them, then they'll operate at a more effective level. In return, I will have more freedom and more money. This isn't a bad thing, though; it's what's called self-profit maximization.

EMBRACE SELF-PROFIT MAXIMIZATION

Do *you* care about your employees? Be honest. No one is looking over your shoulder to judge your answer—it's just you and this book.

If you don't care about your employees, it's okay. Once you acknowledge where you are as a leader, you can make the necessary changes to cultivate a passionate workforce.

Maybe you're like the former version of me, wondering *why* you need to care about your employees. When you get down to the center of the onion, I believe that the point of life is to achieve ethical and moral happiness. It's okay to work toward achieving success and satisfaction, but once you tick those boxes for yourself, it's in your best interest to help others tick their boxes off as well.

I was first introduced to this lesson when my undergraduate philosophy professor said, "Everyone is a self-profit maximizer."

Immediately, half of the class was up in arms. "Philanthropists aren't self-profit maximizers," they argued. "They're selfless with their money."

My classmates were wrong. Even philanthropists are self-profit maximizers. Do you think a philanthropist donates money to a cause and feels *nothing*? No, philanthropists donate money to causes because doing so helps them feel good. They feel a higher level of happiness when they use their money to help others. Also, philanthropists cannot engage in philanthropy without first acquiring the wealth to do so.

We need to reclaim the word "selfish" and embrace the term "self-profit maximization." Ultimately, self-profit maximization is about accomplishing your goals so you can help others accomplish their goals.

So, let's start with ourselves. Everyone has six areas, generally, where they want to achieve success:

- Safety
- Financial security
- Health
- Friendships
- Romantic relationships
- Spirituality

Success in no single area will result in happiness; they're all essential. However, if you manage to achieve success in all of them, you'll generally feel happy, except in difficult moments like the loss of a family member. Even then, you'll have the support to recover.

I believe I'm doing better than many multimillionaires in Hollywood. Why? It is because not only are my wife and I able to afford new experiences and not stress over our bills, but I'm also happy with my family, where I live, my religious faith, my health, and my freedom to safely speak my mind. Someone like Mel Gibson or Johnny Depp might be extraordinarily rich, but we've learned from the tabloids the turmoil they have been, and very well may be, continuing to deal with. I would argue that even though they're making tons of money, they're missing the bigger picture.

Once you, like me, achieve your definition of success and happiness, you can start to shine the spotlight on someone else. You pivot from being self-focused to being other-focused.

For example, Scott Harrison was a promoter who spent all of his time in clubs—drinking, doing drugs, and smoking cigarettes. When he finally decided to fix his life, he quit his job, packed his bags, and went to Africa to become a photographer. There, he encountered many people with physical deformities and wondered, *Why is this happening?*

Harrison learned that people in certain areas only had access to water that was infested with parasites. Moved, he founded Charity Water, an organization focused on funding the drilling of wells that provide these people with access to fresh water.

Watching water shoot out of the ground isn't very exciting for most of us, but imagine what it must have felt like for Harrison to see the locals dancing around like they'd just won the lottery as fresh water surged forth from the earth. Using your own success as a platform from which you can help others transforms and multiplies your personal happiness. Then, when those people check off their own boxes, they give to others too. None of these acts are selfless, but their benefits compound.

Remember, though, that care has to be genuine. If you're insincere, people will feel condescended or pandered to.

Somebody once told me if you want loyalty, do something for someone's kid. If you're a parent, then you know you'd lose your mind if someone abused your child, and at the same time, if someone went out of their way to do something nice for your child, you'd feel extreme positivity toward them. With that in mind, I send a birthday card and a gift to all of my employees' children who are under the age of eighteen. Communicating that you care doesn't have to be expensive.

Similarly, my father taught me you don't have to do a lot more than everybody else; you just have to do a little more. For example, my competition is other companies, so I'm always trying to figure out how they treat their employees and what I can do that's a little bit better. I can't pay everyone $500,000 a year or make their lives completely painless, but I can look for opportunities to improve their work experience—and provide the business a return on investment.

REFLECT ON YOUR WORKFORCE

Before we move on to Chapter 2, consider: Do you spend most of your day putting out fires your employees should be handling? Is your workforce retention rate low? Is there distrust or active conflict between departments? Are you expecting employees to perform exceptionally without providing them the necessary tools or leadership?

Just as doctors can only help their patients when they know what's ailing them, you need to look at your company and find out what symptoms it's exhibiting. Mr. Dube's mistake was in not examining the symptoms of resentment his leadership was causing.

If you haven't already, check out your company's Glassdoor reviews. See what past or present employees have to say about working for you. After all, you are defined by your actions, not your words. How you think of yourself as a leader means nothing if no one perceives you the same way. Perception is reality.

Even if your reviews are good and your operations are running smoothly for the most part, a great leader needs to continuously work to make their company just a *little* bit better. I'm in a constant state of being comfortably uncomfortable. Comfortable, knowing business is going well and things are under control. Uncomfortable, because I know that there is something that I am not currently doing, and if I were doing it, I would be even more efficient and productive.

Find ways to incentivize continuous improvement, and build self-reinforcing positive habits. How are the people you lead improving their industry knowledge, their functional knowledge, and their level of job satisfaction? How can you gamify tasks? What cutting-edge training or system implementation will leverage the talent you lead?

These questions will help you begin to consider what you can tweak and what you can try, to create a thriving, passionate workforce. Now, let's talk more specifically about the Passionate Workforce Spectrum.

CHAPTER 2

THE PASSIONATE WORKFORCE SPECTRUM

"I've learned that people will forget what you said, people will forget what you did, but people will never forget how you made them feel."
—MAYA ANGELOU, POET

In any company, no matter how well you've prepared, it's inevitable that problems will arise. As you begin to reflect on your workforce, you may notice deep-seated issues that you would never have been aware of otherwise. This is a good thing. Awareness of a problem is the first step toward solving it.

However, it's not the last step. Next, you need to search for the root cause of each problem and take corrective action. Understanding where each of your employees fall on a scale from resentful to passionate will be the key to successfully navigating the problems that can otherwise derail a successful business.

CONDUCT ROOT CAUSE ANALYSIS

Operating with an unhappy workforce is akin to leaving port with a significant hole in your ship's hull. Before you can start the necessary repair work, it's important to understand how that hole got there in the first place.

Root cause analysis helps you identify how the holes in your organization got there so that you can adequately address them. It helps you find the true solution to an issue. This is important, because if you leave these situations unaddressed, you'll find yourself with a resentful workforce.

Holes in your ship can look like a lack of curiosity, a lack of openness, or a lack of candor. These qualities affect every part of an employee's day—and even worse, they're often contagious. If the root cause of an issue exists within an employee, it will stay confined to that employee. However, when issues are systemic, they repeat themselves across people, across departments, and over time.

Politicking at the workplace is a common symptom of a systemic problem. It's especially common for departments to form factions against one another. For example, in an unhealthy work environment, the business development team might set unreasonable expectations with a client and then drop the project on the project delivery team's desk, effectively making it their problem. Left unaddressed, systemic problems like this will result in a high turnover rate in your workforce.

A good CEO is defined by their endless curiosity, their need to understand *why*. They are not satisfied with a simple answer.

One way to understand the root cause of a problem is by asking "Why?" five times. For example, a conversation with an employee who showed up late to work might go like this:

Why were you late to work?
I had to stop by the gas station.
Why did you have to stop by the gas station?
I ran out of gas.
Why didn't you fill it up last night?
I didn't have enough time.
Why didn't you have enough time?
I was running around like a chicken with my head cut off because I'm overwhelmed at work. Then I had to pick up the kids from school. Then I had to cook dinner because I'm a single parent.
Why are you so overwhelmed at work?
I've asked for support, but I'm not getting the support that I need. I should be working forty hours, but I'm actually putting in sixty to eighty hours per week.

By peeling back that onion, we just learned something important. We discovered that the employee wasn't late because they're irresponsible but because they're not getting the support they asked for from management.

All conversations with your employees should touch on the personal and professional, so actively listen to understand your audience. Say, "I observed this, and it made me think this. Am I close?" When you're not ready to ask a question or provide a comment, say, "I'm listening" so that they know you are engaged in the conversation.

When you're ready, ask if they have any questions or if there is anything else they would like to share. If so, don't follow up with yes/no questions; ask open-ended questions that prompt them to speak in more detail. Be curious about why they think or feel a certain way.

Let me give you another example of when I used the Five Whys in my business. Earlier in my company's history, I had an employee who approached me and said, "I'd like a raise. And I'm willing to do x, y, and z to get that raise."

At that point in time, I couldn't justify the raise; the company didn't have the money for it. A few weeks later, the employee submitted his resignation, which caught both me and the management team off guard. We didn't get the vibe that the raise was important enough to this person that he would leave if he didn't get it.

In hindsight, we should have conducted a root cause analysis to understand why this employee was asking for more money. Since we didn't, we instead found ourselves stuck in a tricky situation, asking him what he would need in order to stay.

Thankfully, we had established a passionate workforce by this point. Remember, when you nurture a highly passionate work environment, you can attract and keep people at a discount like the New England Patriots did during the 2000s and 2010s. Because the employee really liked working with us, he listened to why we couldn't give him the full raise and agreed to stay for half of what he originally asked for. We were able to keep him for tens of thousands of dollars less than what his other potential employer had offered him.

It's awesome that we were able to save an employee, but that wasn't enough. We also needed to conduct a root cause analysis so that we could avoid a similar situation down the road. Had we done this analysis in the first place, we might have been able to avoid negotiating.

Our internal discussion progressed as follows:
Why were you able to save an employee from leaving?
I was able to give him more money.
Why were you able to give him more money?
I did an analysis on what the cost, time, and effort

would be to find somebody new and train them as a replacement. I learned that giving him the money was justified.

Why were you able to identify the correct number to give him?
He told us his number, and we met him in the middle.

Why was he willing to meet in the middle?
He enjoyed working with the company enough that he would rather stay with us than get paid more somewhere else.

What did you learn from this process?
The next time someone asks for more money, we should take a deeper look into what the reason might be. Then we can determine what's a deal-breaker or not.

Since this conversation, we have realized that one way to maintain a positive workforce is to avoid negotiating salaries. Either your employee gets what they asked for, or they don't and they leave. We will discuss this tip more in Chapter 5, but for now, know that meeting your employee halfway is setting them up for disappointment, which can lead to resentment.

Conducting regular root cause analyses allows you to get to the heart of potential problems and find solutions that create value for you and for your employees. Fewer problems means smoother sailing, which moves employees toward passion.

GET TO KNOW THE THREE TYPES OF EMPLOYEES

There are three types of employees on the Passionate Workforce Spectrum, and you have likely encountered each of them as a leader. Understanding which types of employees you have is crucial to creating the best workforce for your business.

THE RESENTFUL EMPLOYEE

If you want to know what a resentful employee looks like, then just watch the movie *Office Space*. It's a classic.

The main character, Peter, works for a company called Initech that has abysmal communications with employees and doesn't act with the greater good in mind. He tells his colleagues he's "gonna lose it," and in response, one of them cheerfully jokes, "Sounds like somebody's got a case of the Mondays." But it's not just Mondays; Peter hates it there every day.

To fix this feeling, Peter visits a hypnotherapist, who says, "After I snap my fingers, you're not going to care about your job anymore. When I snap again, you *will* care." The therapist snaps once, but before he can snap again, he has a heart attack and dies, which means that Peter is stuck not caring.

When Peter goes back to work, he fools around. He goes fishing, brings the fish he catches to work, and proceeds to gut it on his desk. He knocks over his cubicle and makes a big mess.

When the company brings in consultants to ask Peter about his day, he answers, "I usually come in late, but I go in through the back door so my boss can't see me. Then I stare at my screen for a period of time before I actually decide to do anything. Then I pretend I'm working, but I'm actually not. I do probably about fifteen minutes of serious work a week."

Peter is the quintessential resentful employee, who has a case of the Mondays every day. Resentful employees:

- Are unaware of how to spend their time
- Are inefficient and unproductive
- Are reactive, rather than proactive

- Are unmotivated and require direction at all times
- Turn over quickly
- Are unsatisfied
- Communicate ineffectively
- Breed a hostile work environment
- Feel overworked and stressed out *or* bored and discouraged

At their worst, resentful employees:

- Actively harm the organization and its success
- Lie to colleagues
- Steal from the company

In later chapters, we'll go into more detail about how to move resentful employees toward passion, but first, let's discuss those who are already in the middle of the spectrum: content employees.

THE CONTENT EMPLOYEE

Content employees are B-players. They're doing well, but they make mistakes. Their performance is satisfactory, but you know they have more potential.

A content employee:

- Shows up on time
- Performs adequately but makes mistakes
- Is not at risk of being fired, but you also don't feel the need to reward and recognize them in public
- Is someone you trust most of the time, but you still have to wonder if they're telling you the *whole* truth all of the time

There's nothing wrong with a content employee. You could do fine with them. However, the goal is to take a good employee and make them *great*. If you can stoke passion in content employees, you will have amazing reports who thrive at their job and whom you enjoy being around.

THE PASSIONATE EMPLOYEE

Passionate employees are A-players. They're quality-driven and results-oriented, excited about helping the company and their coworkers grow.

A passionate employee:

- Shows up early
- Responds with urgency
- Is enthusiastic and optimistic
- Is respectfully candid
- Finds creative and innovative ways to accomplish tasks
- Is both confident and humble
- Feels empowered to reach out and ask for help
- Feels empowered to assist their coworkers
- Feels a sense of ownership in the organization

In short, passionate employees are a positive influence in any organization. You want a workforce full of these kinds of people—and a good place to start is with a Passionate Workforce Assessment.

PERFORM A PASSIONATE WORKFORCE ASSESSMENT

The Passionate Workforce Assessment is designed to show you where each employee in your company falls along the

Passionate Workforce Spectrum. It also offers clear direction on specific pillars that require attention, both holistically and on a case-by-case basis.

To begin, have your team members rate how well you perform each of the 15 Pillars on a scale from zero to ten, with zero representing strong disagreement and ten representing strong agreement. I will explain the reasoning behind each of these pillars in more detail in Chapter 5, but for now, I've listed them for your convenience:

- Pillar #1: Give Clear Direction
- Pillar #2: Provide the Necessary Tools to Complete the Job
- Pillar #3: Empower Employees to Make Decisions on Their Own
- Pillar #4: Operate with the Greater Good in Mind
- Pillar #5: Respect Employees' Bandwidth
- Pillar #6: Set Clear Expectations
- Pillar #7: Communicate Respectfully and Candidly
- Pillar #8: Determine an Acceptable Team Meeting Cadence
- Pillar #9: Conduct Regular One-on-One Meetings
- Pillar #10: Offer Rewards and Recognition
- Pillar #11: Assess Employees' Job Satisfaction
- Pillar #12: Cultivate Strong, Resilient Relationships
- Pillar #13: Ensure Employees Feel a Sense of Purpose
- Pillar #14: Compensate Your Workforce Appropriately
- Pillar #15: Achieve a Good Work–Life Blend

Once your employees finish the assessment, average all their answers to determine where they are on the Passionate Workforce Spectrum:

- 0–6: Resentful
- 7–8: Content
- 9–10: Passionate

If someone rates one of the 15 Pillars lower than a 7, you need to take corrective actions immediately. One way to start is to average everyone's scores for each of the 15 Pillars to determine which areas you need to improve. We will get into the specifics of how you can implement these improvements in the following chapters.

SOLVE PROBLEMS WITH PASSION

Passionate employees point out problems before anyone else notices them. Some leaders might look at those problems and think they're not worth addressing, but you want to treat problems that are the size of a grain of rice like they're bombs. You know that, left unaddressed, they can explode.

To avoid problems becoming a source of resentment, let your employees know that you don't care how small they perceive their frustrations to be. You want to identify the root cause of their frustration, discuss it, and resolve it so it disappears forever. This doesn't mean that every employee always gets their way, but when you address their issues in good faith, mutually favorable resolutions are almost always possible.

CHAPTER 3

PRIMING YOUR NEW HIRES FOR LONG-TERM PASSION

"Changes that seem small and unimportant at first will compound and turn into remarkable results if you're willing to stick with them for years."

—JAMES CLEAR, *ATOMIC HABITS*

Back in the day, if you worked for a company for decades, they'd give you a gold watch when you retired. People say that PepsiCo. started this tradition in the 1940s, but whoever did, it became a symbol for the pinnacle of a person's career. *You gave us your time; now we give you ours.*

Well, it's not the 1940s anymore. People won't stay at the same company for their whole career if they aren't passionate about their job, so you have to foster passion early. From writing a job description to conducting interviews, you should make candidates want to support your company's goals before they even sign on. After all, if you pick the right person for the right seat, 90 percent of the management required has already taken care of itself.

THINK OF THE HIRING PROCESS LIKE DATING

Pretend your company is you. You're trying to figure out if the person that's sitting across the table is the right fit for you, but at the same time, you're trying to make yourself seem very attractive.

It doesn't matter that you don't yet know whether you're going to date them. It's in your best interest to get them excited about you because if you decide you do want a romantic relationship, you don't want them to choose someone else.

NAVIGATE THE FIRST DATE

In dating and in job interviews, first impressions matter. When you look at a group of candidates, you remember who you have a good feeling about. Similarly, candidates remember the companies they have a good feeling about.

So, during the interview, make the conversation matter. Don't stick to standard small talk. Asking someone to tell you about their experience or how they would handle a specific situation is like talking about the weather. It's boring—and not very meaningful. You can talk about the weather, but you should also dig in deeper.

Just like in dating, you don't want to pursue someone who doesn't match what you're looking for. If you're looking for a long-term hire, for example, it's important you find out whether this person is looking for something long-term. Find out why they're making a career move and see if you can give them what they want.

Most people will say they want to further their career, but what do they mean by that? Do they want to work independently? Were they being micromanaged in their last role? Was the commute terrible? Were they not paid enough? There are so many different factors that result in people wanting to find a new job.

You should also make the interview a two-way conversation. Communicate that you understand the common frustrations employees have with leaders and managers. Touch on the things that you believe your organization can solve for them.

Let's say this person was overworked in their last job. You could say, "Well, we don't care about 'butts in seats'; we care about the job getting done. So, we don't care how you organize your time—if you take a long lunch or leave early to rest at home—as long as you respond with urgency."

You should then educate them on the plight of the employer. Employees often expect their leaders and managers to know everything that's going on, so they sometimes don't raise issues, especially if they feel voiceless in the workplace.

I tell candidates that we don't encourage people to speak up, we require it. I know generally what a person does, but I don't always know the specifics. When I hire someone, I do so because I trust them to execute on activities and to innovate solutions.

"Throwing people under the bus" is not a phrase we use or believe in. It's everyone's job to hold each other accountable. When there's a problem, employees should start with an inquiry; if they don't see a behavior change, they should do a root cause analysis and provide recommendations, if needed. The final step is to escalate the issue to the employer. After all, CEOs should be focused on selling their business, not taking orders, writing proposals, or dealing with interpersonal issues.

A journey of a million miles starts with one step. So, start cultivating passion within potential new hires from the first interview. Then, once you've gotten to know each other a bit, introduce them to your friends.

INTRODUCE THEM TO FRIENDS

As part of the hiring process, candidates interview with more than one person. Usually, these interviews start with a recruiter, then a hiring manager or the person they would report to. Then the candidate might speak with a lateral manager in a different department or even a colleague they might end up working with side by side.

Having multiple interviews is pretty standard, but you may not realize that it's an important part of fostering passion. When a candidate hears the same story over and over again, from multiple people in the company, they think, *Everybody seems really happy.* Hearing consistent responses helps the candidate believe their impression of the work environment is not too good to be true. Your company might actually be a great place for them.

It's like introducing someone you're seeing to your friends. Suddenly their perception of you is corroborated (or not) by how your friends talk about you. *Oh, Nick? He's great! We've been friends for years, and he's always been there for me.*

That's the thing about a passionate workforce. When they're passionate, they happily advocate for the company.

It's also an important part of your assessment of the candidate. In their conversations, your colleagues might see red flags or potential that you missed. Getting multiple people's perspectives empowers the employer to make the right hire.

COURT AND BE COURTED

Advocating for your company to a candidate doesn't mean you should give out Lindor truffles and relaxing massages. Don't just keep courting them and telling them how great it is to work for your company. Challenge them to court you back. You may have a positive work environment, but it should still be a serious environment.

Candidates can court you back by putting in some sweat equity. Think of sweat equity like this: I have a house I want to sell, but it needs renovations. So, I change the carpet, paint the walls, and build a patio in the backyard—I put my sweat and labor into the renovations. The more time and effort I put into the renovations, the more I value the renovations made. Similarly, the more time a candidate invests into the interview process, the more they value the position they are applying for.

Here are a few examples of what you could have candidates do:

- Create a full presentation pertinent to their potential future workload
- Draft a document they would typically create or work with in your company
- Take skill assessments (relevant technologies, aptitude in skills, etc.)
- Take personality assessments

You don't want candidates to invest a ton of time. If you ask for an unreasonable amount of work before they're even hired, they'll wonder what you'll demand after. However, it should take enough time and effort that they sweat a little bit.

If a candidate doesn't bow out between the sweat equity

and multiple rounds of interviews, they'll lean in further. They won't want all their stress to be for nothing, so they'll subconsciously justify the time and effort they've put into applying to your company. This fosters passion.

MOVE IN TOGETHER

Let's say the calls with a potential hire go well, and they ace every interview. By this point, they know what the pay is, what the responsibilities are, and everything else the job entails. They're just waiting for that final call.

If you're ready for them to move in, someone high up should make the call: the CEO, the VP, etc. Regardless of who calls, they shouldn't just offer them the job. They should ask, "What would you like to have happen?"

The candidate will answer, "I'd really like to get hired."

Then the higher-up will have the chance to respond, "Okay, you got the job."

Think about the level of excitement that statement can generate. The candidate basically gets to speak what they want into existence.

Once they're hired, it's time for them to move in. So, start by celebrating!

Celebrate Your New Hire

The first thing you should do when you hire someone is celebrate. You can throw them an actual party, but any kind of celebratory welcome will work.

For example, have them fill out a "get to know you" sheet. What's their favorite color? What's their favorite food? What kind of activities do they like? Send that sheet to everybody in the department they're joining. This allows the new hire to develop connections with their colleagues before they even start.

"Oh, you like motorcycles? I love motorcycles!"

"Oh, you went to UMass in 1999? I went to UMass in 1999!"

Their favorite candy is black licorice? Give them hell! "Hey, Kelly, I was really excited about you being hired until I found out you like black licorice."

Have fun with it.

It's also a good idea to send your new hire a personalized welcome gift on their first day. If they love going to the spa, get them soaps and shampoos. If they're obsessed with their dog, get them a little doggy sweater. Show them you put thought into the gift; if you just send them a card with a candle, it'll have little to no impact on them.

When people come home, they usually take their shoes off and talk about their day at work with their loved ones. If a new hire hated their job, they'd probably just complain, but imagine if they received a welcome gift on their first day. *Look, honey, my boss gave me a sweater for Rascal!* Gestures like that plant the seeds of passion.

It's easier to stoke passion from the outset than it is to reignite it after it's dead. Once you've got the fire going, you just need to maintain it to keep it alive.

Schedule One-on-Ones

Whenever you move in with someone, that first week is usually a weird dance as you try to figure each other out. You've each got to learn the rules of the space, who takes care of what, how things get done and where, all that.

For a new hire, that "first week" is the training period. The length of that period will differ for every company, but it should cover all the basics: what the company does, what the person's job function is, how they do their job, and what they need to know in order to do it.

During the training period, new hires should have the chance to schedule one-on-ones with everyone who received their "get to know you" sheet. That way, they can build a community and establish a sense of camaraderie immediately.

The timing is important. You want to almost overwhelm them with happiness so that you're constantly reinforcing passion.

I just got the job! I got this amazing welcome gift. I spoke to Mike, and we have this in common. I spoke to Alan, and we have this other thing in common. I'm making so many good connections, and this is just my first week.

If you do this, the new hire will quickly feel secure in their role. They'll feel a sense of support and know who to turn to for what. They'll realize you're reinforcing everything they heard during the interview process, and they'll think, *No, this isn't too good to be true. I'm going to like it here.*

TRAINING BREAKS

Don't overwhelm new hires with information during training. After a certain point, it can feel like drinking from a fire hose. Generally speaking, structure their days like this: one hour training, one hour break, one hour training, one hour break, and so on and so forth.

Take the time to check in with new hires and see how they're doing. If they answer, "I'm feeling overloaded, actually. Would it be okay if we push this one out a little bit?" you should respond, "No problem." Why train them if they can't hear it? It'd be pointless. This goes back to understanding the plight of the employee; leaders and managers might think employees don't have a limit, but they do.

The training period will inherently be challenging for a new hire because they're basically entering a whole new world. Every move could cause them to become resentful, so plan ahead. Make them feel safe.

GET THEM RAMPED UP

There is always a period of time, usually thirty to ninety days, between when an employee finishes training and when they're fully integrated. I call this the "ramp-up period."

During this ramp-up period, have your new hire join their department's weekly meetings, but don't give them any goals. Not a single one. Just have them track how they do compared to a predetermined set of measurables. *Hey, here's five to seven metrics you and your colleagues get measured on. You don't have any goals. Just come in and report your numbers.*

For example, if the new hire is in a sales position, every week have them report the number of calls they made, how many emails they sent out, how many proposals they sent out, how many deals they closed, whatever is relevant to their position. At your next quarterly meeting, review how they did the previous quarter and then have them create their first goals. They need their own goal. Do not allow them to accept some arbitrary goal from somebody else.

If I tell Lisa she has to hit $2 million this quarter, any time she runs into a roadblock, she'll think, *Screw Nick for giving me this impossible goal.* However, if she sets a goal for herself and knows she has support whenever challenges show up, she will work harder. Leadership plus management equals accountability.

The cool part is that at this point, the new hire has gotten to hear everyone else's numbers at the weekly meetings throughout the quarter. They have a sense of what is average, so you can comfortably say, "Hey, Jeff, you've been here for two months. These are the numbers you've been reporting. This is going to be your first full quarter. We're all setting goals. What do you think you can do in terms of revenue?"

Jeff might think, *I don't want to say $100,000 because I know I could do more. Also, I don't want to say $1 million because I know I'd miss that and look like an idiot.* Then he'll look at you and say, "I can do $450,000."

Most of the time, the goal a new hire sets for themselves will be acceptable. However, if it seems too low or too high, you can try to shepherd them toward a different number. Ask why they think that goal is appropriate. Make suggestions using a historical range for new hires. But remember, you're just trying to grease the skids.

Once you and the new hire settle on a number together, hold them to it. They should track their progress every week. Then at the end of the next quarter, check in and see if they hit their goal.

KEEP THE PASSION ALIVE

When you prime new hires for long-term passion, you eliminate countless branching paths of frustration that could crop up down the line. As we've discussed, it's easier to maintain a passionate workforce because your new hires *start* passionate. They don't stumble their way into passion; you encourage and cultivate it.

However, you need to keep that spark alive. Like maintaining any relationship, romantic or otherwise, maintaining a passionate workforce takes effort. Otherwise, people get frustrated.

Keep this truth in mind: if you aren't moving forward, you're moving backward.

CHAPTER 4

HOW TO KEEP YOUR WORKFORCE PASSIONATE

"Make sure that you are seeing each person on your team with fresh eyes every day. People evolve, and so your relationships must evolve with them. Care personally; don't put people in boxes and leave them there."

—KIM MALONE SCOTT, *RADICAL CANDOR*

It's one thing to get a flame started, and it is another thing to keep it going. For you to maintain a flame, you need to feed it and protect it from threats.

Passion is a flame, and goodwill is the oil you feed it. Frustration is the wind that threatens to blow out passion, turning it into resentment.

There are a number of ways you can feed and defend passion in your long-term employees. In this chapter, we will discuss the practices I've found most effective in my own work. Implement and adapt those you find most useful for your company.

IMPLEMENT UNLIMITED PAID TIME OFF

Everyone knows that staying at your job when there's nothing to do is meaningless, but taking time off for no reason is also meaningless. When you have three to four weeks of vacation in a year under a "use it or lose it" policy, for example, you feel like you'll lose something if you don't use it. You enter a scarcity mindset. So, what do you do? You wait until December to take two weeks off, and then you sit on your couch all day and eat crackers and cheese. Are you really happier doing that?

Let's be honest: under a "use it or lose it" policy, it's almost like your company forces you to take the time off. That kind of approach to paid time off perpetuates contentment at its best and creates resentment at its worst.

Time is our most valuable resource, so offering employees unlimited paid time off inevitably stokes the flame of passion. In fact, studies show that giving employees agency over their time leads to increased happiness.

When employees don't feel they have agency over their time, they might stare at a screen all day to save up their paid time off, only to waste their time off at the end of the year doing nothing at home. When employees have agency, however, they become more intentional about their time.

Plus, studies have found that with unlimited paid time off, people actually *work more* and *take off less*. This is the natural outcome of passionate people being able to work when they want and rest when they want.

With unlimited paid time off, I can take an amazing trip abroad and actually enjoy my time. When December comes, instead of burning through two weeks of time for no reason, I can work because I *want* to work. Because there's stuff for me to do. Also, there's the flexibility for me to take off a few hours early if I want to.

Is there the opportunity for abuse with unlimited paid time off? Absolutely. But only from resentful employees. Once you've established a passionate workforce, you don't need to be concerned about exploitative behavior.

This doesn't mean you shouldn't plan for the worst case scenario; you should. Create an unlimited paid time off policy with specific parameters. For instance, employees can't take every Friday off or take paternity leave for two years.

Unlimited paid time off is about allowing employees to control their time.

CHOOSE PROFIT-SHARING

From the very beginning, my company has engaged in profit sharing, and it's proven to be instrumental in developing a passionate workforce. Interestingly, this success seems to be as much about the frustration that a typical merit-based compensation program creates as it is about the passion that a profit-sharing program creates.

Let's talk about what a typical merit-based compensation program looks like versus a profit-sharing program.

MERIT-BASED COMPENSATION

When a company has a merit-based compensation program, employees want to sell as much as they can. They have a scarcity mindset, believing that if they're not making money, they're losing money. They don't want their colleagues to succeed because they're looking out for themselves—not the company.

When there's competition between people who are on the same team, resentment grows. Maybe John is bitter because he was given a crappy territory. Or maybe he thinks leadership is playing favorites because all the big deals are given to Shelley.

Let's say John lands a big deal. Because his colleagues also have a scarcity mindset, they spend their time trying to weasel their way into his deal. Shelley, for instance, says, "I first called them six months ago—that should be my deal." So, now John is bickering with Shelley, and the boss has to take time out of his day to settle the issue.

All this competition between colleagues creates politicking. Shelley and John race to rub elbows with their recruiter and offer to take them out to lunch. They're focused on being manipulative to achieve their own success.

Do you think employees care about the well-being of their company when they have a scarcity mindset? No. They don't care about how much money the company spends because that's not how they make their money; they make money based on revenue from their deals.

So, if somebody asked John, "Hey, should we go to this conference? Should we buy this advertisement? Should we pay for this sales trip?" he would answer, "Yes, yes, yes." When employees only keep their own interests in mind, they will take your marketing budget and grow it indefinitely. They will gladly have the company invest $10 million in marketing so they can make $4 million for themselves.

In short, whatever happens to the company matters far less to people like John than how much he sells—even if his actions decrease the company's overall profits. In other words, a merit-based program incentivizes poor decision-making. It almost always encourages workers to find ways to abuse it and exploit it for their own gain.

PROFIT-SHARING COMPENSATION

In a company with a profit-sharing program, politicking, bickering, and frustration are essentially absent. There is no toxic competition, no arguing about favoritism. There's a communal attitude because everyone knows if the company succeeds, they all reap the rewards, and, if the company fails, they all share the same pains. Everyone's thinking shifts from *How can I ensure my success?* to *How can I ensure the company's success?* because the company's success *is* the individual's success.

In a profit-sharing environment, employees make decisions in the best interest of the company. Tim, for instance, doesn't want the company to spend $10,000 on a single ad or $20,000 to send him to a conference if those decisions don't feed the company's bottom line. After all, if the company loses money, so does Tim.

In fact, if the company starts to tank or run into roadblocks, employees are now incentivized to be innovative and creative. Reports will discuss strategies to get the company's numbers up and even start holding each other accountable. They'll reach out to their colleagues and say, "Hey, you seem to be struggling. I'm here to help you out. What can I do for you?"

In a merit-based program, at best, employees don't care if their colleagues are failing, and at worst, they want them to fail. In a profit-sharing program, everyone cares about everyone's performance. If Stacy is not doing her job well, for instance, it affects Tim; it affects the whole company. If Tim is not doing his job well, it affects Stacy; it affects the whole company. It's in everyone's best interest to make sure their colleagues are performing well—and to speak up when they're not.

If Stacy reaches out to Tim and says, "Hey, do you need

any help? I noticed you haven't been hitting your numbers lately," Tim can't respond, "Thanks, Stacy, but it's none of your business." His performance *is* her business because it affects her and everyone else's compensation.

Let me reiterate. Profit-sharing is not a "get out jail free" card; performance still matters. If an employee is not carrying their weight or contributing to the company's success, it's in everyone's best interest to let go of that person.

A common concern from leaders and managers is that if you don't pay people based on how much they sell, they won't have the motivation to sell. That's not true. Studies show that only a small percentage of salespeople work harder for money. The majority of salespeople work harder for recognition—because they want to be at the top of the scoreboard. Money is just the proverbial cherry on top.

In a profit-sharing environment, you still get the scoreboard competition. When Tim's doing great, Stacy's not bitter about him getting more money. However, she is certainly motivated because she wants to be the one at the top of the scoreboard and get that recognition.

Likewise, Tim is not upset if the boss gives Stacy all the "good" deals because he recognizes Stacy's really good at big, complicated deals. She deserves them. Tim can take care of other deals that suit him, and neither of them feel overworked. In this environment, frustration dissipates, allowing room for healthy competition.

Let's take it one step further. Stacy can ask for Tim's help on a deal without having to worry about losing out on money. They're not splitting commission on it like they would under a merit-based program. So, now Tim is incentivized to help her because if she can land the deal, they both make more money.

At my company, I commonly get requests for salary increases, but I almost never receive requests to increase percentages of profit-sharing. If you asked me why, I would say it's because of that communal attitude I talked about before. The team comes to view profit-sharing as each of them getting a slice of the pie—if they took a bigger slice, it would take away from someone else's slice.

That's just pure speculation, though. What I know for sure is that people are really happy to get those bonus checks. If the company is making a lot of money, then everyone in the company is too. If the company is not making a lot of money, then it is the same for everyone else. Profit-sharing eliminates the "woe is me" mentality because shared profit equals shared fate.

LOGISTICS OF PROFIT-SHARING

Without going into the nitty-gritty of the many ways to successfully implement profit-sharing at your organization, let's examine some of the key details you should remember. First, it's important for *everyone* in the company to benefit from profit-sharing. Not everyone's going to get the same percentage, but everyone gets a slice of the pie. And I mean everyone—janitors, salespeople, cafeteria workers, HR, executives, etc.

Let's say you think you can get away with excluding the janitor. If you think he doesn't know what everybody else makes, then you're kidding yourself. Not only will he feel left out, he'll also feel like a second-class citizen. So guess what? He won't clean the floor as well as he should. He won't clean the toilets as well as he should. He won't do as well as he should because he feels unappreciated and undervalued.

He'll become resentful because everyone is getting bonuses except for him.

However, if the janitor is included in the profit-sharing, he'll take pride in the details, like spending a little extra time getting specks off the mirrors. We all know that clean, pleasant-smelling bathrooms are awesome. Even if they don't put a pep in your step, they prevent the frustration of dealing with a horribly maintained bathroom. They have a positive impact.

The CEO will determine how much of the company's profit they want to give back to the workforce. If they say 1 percent, then good luck finding anybody. If they say 90 percent, then the company's not going to make enough profit. But it's really up to each CEO how they want to handle it.

Whatever percentage the CEO lands on is then divided among all the employees, but there are levels to the profit dictated by position. So what the CEO gets is not the same as what the vice presidents get, which is not the same as what the directors get, which is not the same as what the managers get, and so on and so forth, but everyone gets something. And everyone will see an increase or decrease in their pay depending on how the company performs.

Here's the long and short of it: profit-sharing eliminates the frustration and toxic competition of merit-based programs. So, it's in your best interest to institute profit-sharing at your workplace.

However, entrepreneurial know-how, like determining what percentage of a company's profit to share, is only part of what makes a leader successful. Another part, as we've touched on, is communicating well—and that includes coordinating productive meetings.

COORDINATE PRODUCTIVE MEETINGS

You've been in terrible meetings before. Meetings that are unstructured and completely off the wall. Random ad hoc meetings that cause a lot of disruption and anxiety.

Imagine walking into a conference room and hearing low murmurs. Everyone's a little bit confused or concerned because they don't know what the meeting is about. Is the company in trouble? Are layoffs happening? Arms are crossed, brows are furrowed, foreheads are being rubbed to assuage people's growing headaches.

Then the boss walks in and puts the spotlight on *you*. You try to answer their questions, but you don't have the answers because they never told you what to expect. People are distracted. Colleagues lose focus. The whole room goes silent as people don't really know how to move forward. It's awful.

The lack of structure, process, and diligence creates frustration in employees because you all know this is inefficient. It's a waste of time—nothing is getting done. You start to lose respect and confidence in the people who are in charge of the company. It's difficult to be excited about a company when you see it's a mess.

Yeah, those kinds of meetings have no place in a passionate workforce. When you come into a meeting that's high-performing, well-organized, and structured, there are no crossed arms, furrowed brows, or growing headaches. In fact, there's laughter and camaraderie. You feel confident and passionate. You can feel the wheels of progress turning.

However, scheduling too many, too few, or unanticipated meetings can lead to frustration among your employees. So, let's look at some ways to ensure that meetings foster passion rather than burn out your workforce.

QUARTERLY AND ANNUAL MEETINGS

If you're not holding quarterly and annual meetings, then you're not doing any planning. All you're doing is working *in* the business, rather than working *on* the business. As much as you have to execute, you also have to strategize.

Think of it like football. You go into the game with a strategy. You play through four quarters, and between quarters, your coach says, "Hey, this is everything we did well out on the field. Here's everything we didn't do so well out on the field." You take that information, readjust your game plan, and apply it to the next quarter. That's the quarterly meeting.

At the end of the game, you see the score. You celebrate a win or evaluate a loss. Then, you strategize for the next game. That's the annual meeting.

When you have quarterly meetings, which should last one day, reflect on the previous quarter: Were we able to hit these numbers? Were we able to reach our goals? Or was the quarter mediocre—or even terrible?

It's important to engage the IDS process here. Identify: what was the root cause of any goal we missed? Discuss: what are some ways we can resolve this problem? Solve: what strategy can we use to take the company to the next level? When you come out of this meeting, everyone should feel energized because you've got a plan for the next quarter.

The annual meeting looks a lot like the quarterly, except it lasts two days and involves reflecting on the previous year and strategizing for the next year. Another key difference is that annual meetings should include a team-building event. You're all people, and you need to bond.

To accelerate bonding, I like to use icebreakers that encourage vulnerability, like "Tell us one thing that nobody in this room knows about you." Typically you've been working with these people for a while, so if they don't know something about you by now, it's probably because it's something you don't want to share. And that is the point. This exercise reminds everyone that we're all human and that we are not perfect. It loosens people up.

In addition to the team-building exercise, I recommend doing something fun. Life is a mixture of melancholy and nirvana, ecstasy and torment, so go go-kart racing or golfing. Rent a house on a lake and go boating. The annual meeting is a really good opportunity for your team to create meaningful, long-lasting relationships, so don't just be there. Be present.

Another big part of team building is love. You don't have to think of your employees as your second family, but you should want to love them and want them to love you. These relationships improve the quality of your life.

Ask yourself: What would it be like if you loved your team? If you knew their history, knew their pain, knew their vulnerabilities? What if they knew your history, your pain, and your vulnerabilities? Above all else, sharing human experiences is an effective way to nurture passion in your workforce.

Long-Term Issues

Long-term issues, once resolved, typically will result in projects that take more than a week or two to complete, such as implementing new accounting software. Everything you missed in the previous quarter should go on this list.

During the quarterly meeting, the Long-Term Issues List goes through the Keep, Kill, Combine exercise. If an issue is still relevant, keep it on the list. If it's not an issue anymore, kill it from the list. If you realize two items on the list are related, combine them.

Finally, you have to determine whether the remaining projects can get moved to the Short-Term To-Do List (e.g., updating the holiday calendar)—which we'll discuss in the next section about the Weekly Meeting—or if they require further planning (e.g., undergoing renovations). If a project is still not complete by the next quarter, it will go through this process again.

Rocks

There's a story about a professor who brought a mason jar into his class and filled it with rocks. He asked the class, "Is this full?" and they said, "Yes." He added some pebbles, which fit between the rocks, and then asked, "Okay, now is it full?" Everybody said, "Yes." Then he poured sand into the jar, which got in between all the pebbles. He asked, "Okay, now is it full?" They all, again, said, "Yes". Finally, he poured water into the jar and said, "Okay, now it's actually full."

The water represents day-to-day things, and the rocks represent important projects. If you overvalue the day-to-day things and fill up the whole mason jar with water, you won't be able to get any rocks in there. You'll neglect the most important projects. So, start with the rocks.

Every quarter, you need to help employees identify the top three to seven things they must complete. These are their rocks, and they will be updated/changed each quarter.

(After ninety days, people's tanks run low. Their motivation wanes. Orienting employees in a ninety-day world keeps them sharp and focused.)

Let's revisit Jeff from Chapter 3. His quarterly rock—or goal—was hitting $450,000. Now, in a fake perfect world, he'd hit $450,000 exactly. In a real perfect world, he would probably hit *just* over $450,000—something like $475,000 or $500,000. But if he said $450,000 and hit $1 million, then you'd know he was sandbagging; if he didn't hit his goal, then it would get marked as incomplete.

In the following section, about weekly meetings, we'll see how the quarterly rocks get reviewed every week.

Weekly Meetings

If you want to stop having terrible meetings, I recommend employing weekly meetings in your organization. The Weekly Meeting is a structured, ninety-minute meeting designed to optimize your team's time.

As we will discuss further in the next chapter, there shouldn't be more than six people in a Weekly Meeting. Otherwise you end up with too many cooks in the kitchen.

Here is the structure for a Weekly Meeting:

- Segue
- Scorecard
- Rock Review
- Headlines
- Short-Term To-Dos
- Short-Term Issues
- Conclude

Let's go over each of these.

Segue (Five to Fifteen Minutes)

Start off by having everyone share good news from their personal and professional lives. For example, "My brother's getting married on Monday," or "We just closed $2 million in two weeks." Starting with good news helps everyone loosen up before you jump into the nitty gritty.

Sometimes people will choose to share bad news instead, like a family member passing, but that's okay. Giving them the space to do so reminds everyone that you're all humans dealing with things together.

Once everyone has a chance to share, move on to reviewing everyone's scorecard.

Scorecard (Five Minutes)

In a company with unlimited time off and no fixed hours of operation, there has to be a mechanism for making sure people get their work done. Measurables or Key Performance Indicators (KPIs) allow you to do that.

Every employee should set their own goals in their quarterly meetings, which we will go over in detail in the next section of this chapter, and those goals should be approved by their leaders or managers. There are also typically five to seven measurables set by the executive team at those quarterly meetings, such as revenue, proposals sent, calls made, number of referrals, and so on.

Week to week, track everyone's progress on both self-selected and assigned measurables. That way, you'll be able to recognize people when they're blazing ahead and nudge people in the right direction when they're behind. Then, at the end of the quarter, everybody will come together and review how they did.

The review is simple: someone either gets a "complete" or "not complete," depending on whether or not they hit their goal. If it's someone's first quarter, it shouldn't be surprising if they don't hit their goal. However, even for a seasoned employee, missing the mark one quarter is not the end of the world. If they miss their goal for several quarters in a row, though, you've got a problem.

Quarterly results are only part of a person's success; it is not everything. As Dannie Ainge said when he was general manager for the Boston Celtics, "You can't control the scoreboard; you can only put yourself in the best position to influence the scoreboard." If you completely ignore the numbers, you are doing your company a disservice. But if you hold quarterly results as gospel, you will most certainly make counterproductive decisions.

If that sounds like a tough needle to thread, remember: the great thing about a passionate workforce is that people *want* to perform well. They want to stay in this positive environment where there's passionate colleagues and unlimited time off and all these other great aspects, so they know they've got to produce.

Now, choosing measurables is always a work in progress. It's one of the hardest things to do as a leader or manager because the measurables you use will change as the company grows. Do not create measurables for the sake of creating measurables. Create measurables for the sake of gathering information that can lead to informed decision-making. If you're capturing a measurable and it's not having any influence on your decision-making, then it's bogus information and it needs to be eliminated.

After addressing each person's scorecard, go into Headlines, or the big things that have happened over the past week in the company.

Headlines (Five to Fifteen Minutes)

Think of Headlines like a highlight reel. This is where you spend a few minutes talking about client updates, such as how the most important projects are going, client satisfaction, deal progress, future opportunities, etc.

It's a great way to get everyone on the same page. And if an issue arises in the Headlines part of the meeting, it gets moved to the Short-Term Issues List, which we'll discuss next.

Short-Term Issues (Fifty to Fifty-Five Minutes)

The Weekly Meeting is a space for employees to safely voice their thoughts, to find the root cause of issues in the workplace, and to solve them. This begins with the Short-Term Issues List.

During the week, if an employee has a question or concern that's not urgent, they write it down on the Short-Term Issues List and put their name beside it. This list should be available to everyone who will attend the Weekly Meeting.

Usually, short-term issues are more than just clarifications. They tend to be bigger problems, like do we approve this person's requested raise? This client wants us to drop our price below what we've said we're willing to do—are we good with that? They can also be opportunities. Should we enter into a new service area or move into a new geographic region? Whether you're dealing with a problem or opportunity, once you come up with a solution, the issue should be added to the Short-Term To-Do List.

Short-Term To-Dos (Five Minutes)

Let's say my company is dealing with a raise request. At the Weekly Meeting, I might say, "Okay, Susannah is requesting an increase in pay. By our next meeting, I will have a call with my superior, and we'll determine whether or not we can approve the request."

Without the Short-Term To-Do List, there's no mechanism for accountability. Let's say for some reason I misunderstood the employee's raise request, and everybody assumed I would take care of it. Without the list, no one would realize it wasn't handled until it became a problem again. With it, the group will make sure to follow up the following week. "Okay, Nick, you were supposed to contact your superior by today and find out whether you can approve the request. What did you find out?"

As long as the appropriate person does their job, you can take the task off the Short-Term To-Do List. Generally speaking, a short-term to-do takes one week, but sometimes it can take longer.

With short-term to-dos, it's important to stay on track. If you jump around from issue to issue, you'll never settle on a course of action, leading to meetings that go on forever without anything actually happening. So, just as you do with long-term to-dos, use IDS. Identify the issue, discuss it, and solve it—so that it goes away forever.

Sometimes you have zero items on the short-term to-do list; other times you have ten or twelve. What's important is that you have that built-in space for employees to address their non-urgent questions and concerns. That way, instead of having an impromptu meeting every time the littlest issue comes up, you have one meeting where you go through all the issues from the past week. This streamlines your communications as a department and as a company.

Conclude (Less than Five Minutes)

At the end of the meeting, everyone rates how it went on a scale from one to ten. You should be earning a ten every meeting.

If you're not, then ask people to explain what would've made it a ten. Maybe someone didn't show up on time. Maybe someone felt disrespected by another colleague. This feedback process offers people the chance to voice any issues that prevented the meeting from being stellar. That way, everyone can keep tabs on those issues in the next meeting.

This accountability is one way to show you truly value your workforce.

STATE OF THE COMPANY

State of the Company addresses are a great way to help employees feel informed and included. In them, you should detail financials, revenue projections, issues with clients, what got completed, and what didn't. You should discuss how the company is doing quarter to quarter and year to year, as well as go in depth on any growth strategies in place. Talk about goals and actuals, gross profit and net profit. Get into the nitty gritty.

What does a State of the Company address have to do with passion? When you engage with your employees in adult conversation, you're acknowledging their humanity. You're showing that you're not hiding any secrets from them. That level of transparency reinforces the idea that the company is acting with the greater good in mind.

There's no use hiding when the company has had a bad quarter. If you pretend that the quarter wasn't as bad as it was, your team will start to lose trust in you. That decreases passion. The State of the Company requires you to be radically candid.

In the absence of truth, human beings create stories, and nine times out of ten, that story is worse than the actual truth. So, if I don't tell you how much money we're making as a company, you'll think we're making more than we actually are and that I'm greedy. If I don't tell you why somebody was let go, you'll come up with your own explanation.

People are primed to think the worst of executives. They expect something nefarious or mischievous behind the scenes. Get ahead of that instinct, and show your reports all the "dirty laundry," even if it's just a bunch of charts and graphs.

The State of the Company is a group huddle, reminding everyone that you are a team. Either you succeed and celebrate together, or you fail and fix things together.

VALUE YOUR WORKFORCE

Keeping your workforce passionate ultimately comes down to implementing policies and processes that consistently show you respect their humanity. That you value them.

Unlimited time off, for instance, shows that you trust your employees to manage their time. Profit-sharing shows that their individual contributions are appreciated and that they're part of a team. Coordinating productive meetings shows that the organization is healthy and that it respects employees' time.

Now that you understand the importance of having a passionate workforce, as well as how to cultivate passion in new hires and maintain it in current employees, it's time to discuss the 15 Pillars. In the next chapter, you'll learn more about the reasoning behind each pillar and how you can use them to maximize your impact.

CHAPTER 5

THE 15 PILLARS OF A PASSIONATE WORKFORCE

"If we want people to fully show up, to bring their whole selves including their unarmored, whole hearts—so that we can innovate, solve problems, and serve people—we have to be vigilant about creating a culture in which people feel safe, seen, heard, and respected."
—Brené Brown, *Dare to Lead*

To become a leader of a human-centered business, you need to focus on employees' needs, both practical and psychological. Remember, you're trying to help them check their boxes so that they are happier and perform better. A passionate workforce results in greater satisfaction and better outcomes for everyone.

The 15 Pillars are a framework you can use to examine your company and make corrective actions as needed. Once again, they are:

- Pillar #1: Give Clear Direction
- Pillar #2: Provide the Necessary Tools to Complete the Job
- Pillar #3: Empower Employees to Make Decisions on Their Own
- Pillar #4: Operate with the Greater Good in Mind
- Pillar #5: Respect Employees' Bandwidth
- Pillar #6: Set Clear Expectations
- Pillar #7: Communicate Respectfully and Candidly
- Pillar #8: Determine an Acceptable Team Meeting Cadence
- Pillar #9: Conduct Regular One-on-One Meetings
- Pillar #10: Offer Rewards and Recognition
- Pillar #11: Assess Employees' Job Satisfaction
- Pillar #12: Cultivate Strong, Resilient Relationships
- Pillar #13: Ensure Employees Feel a Sense of Purpose
- Pillar #14: Compensate the Workforce Appropriately
- Pillar #15: Achieve a Good Work–Life Blend

Now, I will explain each of these pillars in more detail, including giving you actionable tips to successfully adapt and implement them. Heads up: this chapter is longer than any other because it covers a lot of important information, but at the end of it, you'll be better positioned to become a "Champion Leader."

PILLAR #1: GIVE CLEAR DIRECTION

All too often, employees talk about feeling like they're on an island when they start a new position. They get no support and no direction. They have no idea how to access training materials, when their tasks are due, or what their goals should be.

Sadly, this is pretty universal across industries—and even for established employees. It's unreasonable to think your team will magically interpret the precise meaning of a vague statement or command. How can you expect anyone to be successful under these circumstances?

TIP #1: ASK FOR FEEDBACK DURING ONE-ON-ONES

Take advantage of your one-on-ones to understand what your employees need from you. Ask them if you're giving good direction, and when they answer, *really listen.* Listen to connect; don't listen to correct.

If you think you're doing a great job giving your employees clear direction, but they don't feel the same, there are two possibilities:

- You need to give better direction.
- You need to educate your employees about why the direction you've given is adequate.

Employees who do not receive clear direction feel isolated, like they have nowhere to turn for clarity or guidance. That's why Weekly Meetings are vital to the success of a passionate workforce.

Remember, emotions drive every decision. So, if your employees are underperforming, asking crazy questions, and/or giving confusing critiques, figure out why so that you can better understand the situation. Don't have a list of questions ready because sometimes that prevents you from actively listening. When getting feedback, you don't want to hinder the natural ebbs and flows of a conversation by waiting to reply.

TIP #2: UNDERSTAND THAT CLEAR DIRECTION ≠ MICROMANAGEMENT

Do you ask your employees, "Where's this? Why'd you do that?" If so, you are micromanaging, not providing clear direction. Clear direction benefits employees, but micromanaging tells employees that you don't trust them, decreasing their sense of ownership and their ability to make their own decisions.

What can you do instead? Rather than monitoring people's every move, I recommend that you meet with them at least once every two weeks. Give clear direction, confirm they understand, then let them do the job. Let their performance speak for itself, and let them show you what they're capable of.

That means giving your employees enough room to make mistakes so that they can learn and grow. Mutual trust leads to investment, which leads to passion. Your employees will begin to wear that trust like a badge of honor, and in turn, they'll be more innovative, creative, and productive.

When you expect employees to produce results that align with their full value, and you trust them to do so, they will also hold themselves accountable. The more you trust them, the more they'll contribute; the more they contribute, the better they'll feel and the more passionate they'll be about their work. It's a positive feedback loop.

PILLAR #2: PROVIDE THE NECESSARY TOOLS TO COMPLETE THE JOB

Communication with colleagues and clients in my first job out of college was limited. In the morning, I'd read and send emails, and after returning from the field, I'd have a new batch of emails to reply to.

Without the proper tools, I couldn't respond to messages

during the day, so they'd pile up, extending my workday and taking time away from my personal life. In addition, I couldn't access information that would have been helpful in the field. It was frustrating.

That all changed once the company gave me a tool—a Blackberry phone—that allowed me to send and reply to emails while I was in the field. I became much more effective and responsive, and morale rose because my colleagues and I knew we could go home after our last sales call, rather than after facing a backlog of emails.

The necessary tools will look different for every industry. A construction company will need physical tools like forklifts, but a staffing agency will require an Applicant Tracking System (ATS). A company that requires people to drive their own cars for work will need to compensate for mileage.

If you don't provide your employees the necessary tools to complete their job, it will take them longer than it should. I guarantee they'll think something along the lines of *These people are expecting me to do x, y, and z, and they're not giving me what I need to be successful.* These thoughts lead to resentment.

When employees have the right tools, however, they work more efficiently, focusing on maximizing their output instead of just getting by. They take more pride in their work and have less frustration with management.

TIP #1: ALWAYS THINK ABOUT RETURN ON INVESTMENT

As a leader, you want to be open when an employee pitches a tool to you, but you also want to consider the return on investment. Will this tool make the company more money? Will it make the company more efficient? Will it make your team members' lives easier?

As we discussed in Chapter 4, profit-sharing is a great way to ensure return on investment because employees will almost always only recommend tools they think will enhance *their* profit. If something is going to make their life easier, but it will also have a serious impact on profit, they'll think twice about asking for it.

TIP #2: LET IT BE AN ORGANIC PROCESS

You don't need to run around constantly looking for and evaluating new tools. They will be necessary at different points in time, either because there's a deficiency in the organization that would be remedied by a tool or because somebody catches wind of a tool that would increase efficiency.

As needs arise, the right tools will present themselves to you. Like we discussed, employees may present tools to you, but someone might also cold call you about a tool that ends up being perfectly suited to your company's needs. Just be open to investing in the right tool at the right time.

PILLAR #3: EMPOWER EMPLOYEES TO MAKE DECISIONS ON THEIR OWN

Most people aren't used to empowerment in the workplace. When they first get hired, they ask questions like "Can I do this?" or "What do you think I should do about that?"

Just as the President of the United States wouldn't decide whether you should repave your driveway, you shouldn't spend your time handling responsibilities that are not reflective of your position in the organization. So, delegate and elevate. Get the monkey off your back.

TIP #1: ASK YOUR EMPLOYEES WHAT THEY WOULD DO

Often, an employee will reach out to me and say, "Nick, we've got this situation." Then they'll give me a choice between A and B and ask what I want them to do. Invariably, I ask, "What's your recommendation?" It's such a frequent refrain that my assistant, who became accustomed to micromanagement with her previous employer, now says, "I knew you were going to say that."

It might seem like a gimmick, but if I tell people what to do, then I'm coming up with the solution instead of supporting them in reaching it using their own expertise. As a result, I foster dependency, and they don't get the satisfaction, confidence, and growth that results from coming up with a winning idea. Nine times out of ten, their recommendation is what I would have done anyway.

Plus, the next time an employee wonders how to proceed, they'll have a better understanding of what works and what I would agree to. They will have honed their instincts to make the decision on their own or, depending on the gravity or complexity of the situation, will come and talk to me. If they don't have a recommendation, I'll walk them through my thinking; that way, they know how to reason for themselves next time, and I don't just become an answer dispenser.

The more you empower people, the more productive they will be and the more they will level up. The more authority they have over decisions, the less you'll get pummeled with questions and the less you'll feel burned out. It's a win-win.

PILLAR #4: OPERATE WITH THE GREATER GOOD IN MIND

The greater good is about both the company as a collective and the company's impact on the world at large.

Internally, do people feel like you're messing with their compensation plans every year? Has undisclosed, questionable conduct leaked out?

As a leader, you need to show that you see your employees as humans, not tools for capital gain. If you demean or exploit them, they will quickly lose respect for you. My company understands that while executive management meetings are private, we're also not trying to pull a fast one on them; we're sincere about being invested in them.

Externally, do people feel like your organization wants them to pitch smoke and mirrors? It's hard for employees to feel truly passionate when they're not working toward the greater good. Think about it—which company probably stokes more passion, one that sells cancer-causing tobacco or one that works toward curing cancer?

I once sold phone service, and 60 percent of the time when people switched, their phone lines went down during the switchover. As a naive college graduate who was still developing ethical boundaries, I would tell prospective customers that they were going to be fine—and hope they fell in the lucky 40 percent.

Acting with the greater good in mind requires a leader and manager to be genuine about doing good and caring for both their people and the world at large. That is a requirement.

TIP #1: ENCOURAGE INPUT

If you maintain open lines of communication, you can keep your finger on the pulse of how aligned people feel you, they, and the company are with the greater good. You can also solicit their ideas for what to improve.

For instance, using anonymous questionnaires will give

employees the opportunity to express concerns about an individual's or the company's ethics, enabling you to correct the problem. Say a salesperson reports that a product they're supposed to push doesn't actually solve the clients' problems and thus doesn't have the greater good in mind—that's useful information for improving your position in the marketplace and retaining your staff.

Since I encourage two-way dialogue, I often get questioned about my policy proposals, such as requiring a twenty-four-hour turnaround for client requests. Someone might raise their hand and point to three instances when they'd have to take longer than twenty-four hours. Armed with that knowledge, we would have two choices, both of which are ethical: take the twenty-four-hour guarantee out entirely or leave it in with a set of assumptions. For example, "We will provide a twenty-four-hour turnaround unless A, B, or C happens, in which case it could extend to forty-eight hours."

I welcome pushback because I know my employees trust me to operate ethically. I know that they feel safe asking questions and working together to improve our overall performance. We're all working toward the best possible outcome.

TIP #2: ASSUME PEOPLE WILL FIND OUT ABOUT EVERYTHING YOU DO

Is your company being sketchy, or is it being ethical?

As a CEO, assume people will find out about everything you do. Even if a decision is "confidential," it will likely come to light. Once it's exposed, people will determine whether it was ethical, and if it wasn't, it will come back to bite you.

Acting with the assumption that nothing will stay secret

helps you keep the greater good in mind. Fortunately, the more you behave ethically, the easier it becomes. There's a snowball effect for yourself, individuals within the company, and the organization as a whole.

There have been times when I've learned after the fact, by accident, that an employee did something ethical when no one was there to witness it. They had the opportunity to choose between right and wrong, and they chose right because we've cultivated a culture of righteousness and altruism.

TIP #3: BE HUMAN IN BUSINESS

Don't fall into the social media trap of only showing your employees your "perfect" life: cars, cruises, shallow relationships, etc. If you ask people questions about themselves, they'll like you, and if you tell them about yourself in a real way, they'll trust you.

We need to see others' pain just as much as their bliss, so to the extent you feel comfortable, be transparent about your shortcomings. Disclose mistakes you've made in your personal life and professional career.

For example, every time someone asks how I started my company, I explain how I went from an entry-level job at a telecommunications company to a leadership position at a multinational pharmaceutical company. When they invariably say, "Wow, how impressive," I tell them that they should be less impressed by me and more repulsed by the person who thought it was a good idea to make a twenty-three-year-old head of North American Business Development. Needless to say, I made a lot of mistakes and learned a lot of lessons. I share those with them.

So, talk about your kid's learning disability, your chronic

back pain, your struggle to quit smoking. I often share petty disagreements I've had with my wife or my grief for my late father.

Being human in business means don't discredit someone's feelings by telling them not to worry or not to cry. We need all of the emotions—including anger and sadness—so embrace them. Be real with others, and allow them to be real with you.

When you do so, you make them feel safe. Next time they have a problem, they'll come to you because they trust that you'll understand. As we've discussed, that trust will translate into greater passion for and investment in their work.

PILLAR #5: RESPECT EMPLOYEES' BANDWIDTH

Working an unreasonable number of hours is an incredibly common cause of frustration in a workforce, and the price is high: an employee's spouse is upset because they're not around, they feel forced to neglect their kids and health, etc. Some leaders and managers may not think work is affecting their employees' quality of life, but an employee doesn't have to be sleeping at the office to feel overworked. Conversely, if an employee is working only ten hours a week and is given no direction, they know their role is unnecessary; they might decide to start looking for a new position now.

Everyone knows employees fear getting fired, but not every employee realizes business owners fear losing people. If I lose an employee, then I'm straining my remaining workforce even more, further risking retention. My strained workforce might miss the mark for clients, making them unhappy and, as a result, losing their business. Thinking about losing an employee brings nothing but sleepless nights and nausea for a leader.

To avoid that spiral, I practice respectful candor. I explain that if an employee has too much work or not enough work, they'll feel resentful, get burned out or bored, and leave. I encourage them to speak up so I don't lose them, and I assure them that it's safe to do so. Then, when problems with bandwidth arise, I make sure to listen.

TIP #1: KEEP WORKWEEKS AT FORTY HOURS ON AVERAGE

You don't need every employee to work exactly forty hours every week—sometimes they'll work thirty hours, sometimes fifty to sixty—but generally speaking, forty hours should be your target. That way, your employees are neither overworked nor underworked.

If you find out an employee is being underutilized, you can give them more work. Get them cross-trained, involve them in a new project, or have them research something for you. It just can't be meaningless busywork—employees can sniff that out in an instant. If you give them something meaningless to do, it'll just contribute to their frustration. Who wants to do something completely meaningless with their time?

TIP #2: UNDERSTAND SWELLS AND TRAJECTORIES

To effectively respect your employees' bandwidth, you need to understand swells and trajectories. A swell is when somebody's bandwidth is being stretched, but only for the short term; they might have to work extra hard for a month or even a quarter because of unique circumstances, but then things will slow down again. In contrast, a trajectory is when an employee's bandwidth keeps stretching and they have no reason to believe it will return to normal.

I tell my employees that I know what they do in their role, but I don't know what their individual bandwidth looks like, so I need them to keep me informed. If their bandwidth starts to shrink, we need to talk about it to determine whether it's a swell or a trajectory. Sixty hours a week for a week or two is not a systemic failure, but sixty hours a week for the foreseeable future indicates the need to reallocate work or hire another employee.

Educate your employees on the difference between these two situations. That way, when an employee asks you for help because they're overworked, you can see if this is something that truly requires more attention and resources or if it's a challenge they can overcome in the short term.

PILLAR #6: SET CLEAR EXPECTATIONS

From the time a candidate applies and interviews for a job to the time they're onboarding, they should have a clear understanding of the expectations of their job. It's in everyone's best interest for them to have as much clarity as possible regarding the type of environment they're walking into and what they're expected to do. The less clear the job description is, the more frustrated they will be.

This pillar relates to the previous one in that if someone's bandwidth is overloaded, they won't be able to meet expectations. Let's say an employee is expected to turn around certain kinds of reports within forty-eight hours; if they're overwhelmed, they'll start missing deadlines. Likewise, if a senior director is overwhelmed, their two-week one-on-ones may slip, causing a negative trickle-down effect.

Setting clear expectations is one of the most difficult pillars to uphold, but as with other pillars, maintaining open lines of communication will help. Just make sure those communicated expectations are reasonable and sustainable.

TIP #1: USE THE RIGHT MEASURABLES

Whether you call them metrics, measurables, or KPIs, you need something to adequately and fairly measure the competency of your employees to determine whether they are meeting expectations. Identifying the most effective measurables is quite difficult. You don't want to capture data just for the sake of capturing data.

It can take months, even years, to fine-tune your measurables. In fact, they're likely to continually change as the company scales, because new priorities arise and old priorities become obsolete. So, go through your measurables on a quarterly basis to see if they still make sense.

It's also best to make a habit of introducing and explaining the reasoning behind any changes during those quarterly meetings so employees don't feel like you're throwing new things at them out of nowhere. For example, you might say, "We're going to remove these metrics because we're not getting information that allows us to make good assessments. We're going to add in these metrics because we believe they'll enhance our ability to make solid decisions."

THE CHALLENGE OF OPTIMIZING SCORECARDS AND KPIS

In my experience, the most difficult thing in business is establishing a *high-quality* scorecard and KPIs. As people evolve, job descriptions evolve, and expectations shift. If you don't keep your finger on the pulse or if you have a poor mechanism for capturing metrics, then you'll make bad decisions based on irrelevant or inaccurate data. Junk in leads to junk out.

The right measurables will depend on your industry and your specific organization's situation. The important part is to zero in on what data will allow you to optimize your business.

TIP #2: LET EMPLOYEES CREATE THEIR OWN GOALS

As employees mature within the company, they realize that expectations organically increase based on what they've done previously and on what their colleagues are currently doing. No one should have the same goal they had three quarters ago, but it's also important that everyone has the opportunity to create their own goals because doing so fosters accountability. In contrast, if you make a recommendation, they'll likely treat it as a directive.

Let's say you tell an employee that they should sell $2 million this year. If they don't meet that measurable, they'll blame you. If you give them a number that's too low, though, they might feel like you don't think they're capable.

Of course, you can give input. If someone agrees to project-manage X number of clients based on their estimation of bandwidth, you can explain why you think the number seems low, high, or just right. If you agree, then that's the number; if you disagree, then you voice your concerns and either guide them toward something more realistic or push them out of their comfort zone. That said, in a passionate workforce, you'll find you rarely have to adjust someone's goals.

The point is to have a collaborative and consultative approach that, in the end, allows an employee to own the goal instead of simply following your orders. If they miss the target, it will not be because you were unreasonable. You can then work together to understand what happened and what can be improved upon without fostering resentment.

PILLAR #7: COMMUNICATE RESPECTFULLY AND CANDIDLY

The first keyword here is *respectful*. If you're disrespectful toward your employees and colleagues—for example, by yelling, swearing, insulting, acting condescending or dismissive—it will be very difficult to create a personal connection. Being paid more than another person doesn't mean you have permission to be disrespectful toward them. You get what you give, so treat the janitor with the same level of respect as the CEO.

However, don't stop there—you also need to be *candid*. If you're not candid, then your employees aren't going to understand what you need from them. Expectations will become blurry, which will result in frustration.

If everything in the workplace were gumdrops and butterflies, nobody would care about candor, but problems arise all the time, which means difficult conversations have to happen. When they do, speak to employees in a firm, friendly, authoritative, and polite manner. Don't beat around the bush, but do be vulnerable where it makes sense.

TIP #1: TREAT EVERYONE DIFFERENTLY BUT WITH EQUAL RESPECT

Treating everyone differently but with equal respect doesn't mean you need to joke around with each person like they're your best friend. It means you need to treat everyone in a way that makes sense for them.

For example, I don't speak to my wife in the same way I speak to my best friend. At work, I use humor with funny people, but I am more direct with serious people. It's all about respecting the way people prefer to interact.

TIP #2: DON'T BE DISMISSIVE

Sometimes leaders and managers believe they communicate in a respectfully candid manner because they're not swearing at their employees, but they still speak in a condescending or dismissive way. For example, when an employee says, "I really don't feel like I'm getting the direction I need," they respond, "No, you're fine" instead of allaying their fears.

When a leader responds in this way, the employee hears the message that they aren't being taken seriously. That sense of alienation then sets the tone for future engagements. They expect that if they raise a problem in the future, they'll be dismissed again, so they're less likely to bring it up. Over time, they may feel resentful about the lack of support.

Remember, passion and resentment lie on a spectrum; people rarely jump from one end to the other after a single interaction. If you dismiss a passionate employee's concern once, they'll feel temporarily frustrated, but overall, they'll still be happy. If you dismiss them again, they'll start to feel like they're just a number to you, and then the next time, they will probably not even try to communicate their concerns.

Since I'm wholly committed to stoking and maintaining passion among my employees, I encourage them to keep lines of communication open about *everything*. I even give them hyperbolic examples: "You don't like the color of my shirt? Tell me! You don't like the flavor of the coffee in the break room? Tell me!" I won't always respond the way they want me to, but I will absolutely hear them out. I want to communicate that anything bothering them is meaningful.

The only exception to this rule is when people complain constantly. When someone communicates their unhappiness about every aspect of the job and the organization, you can assume they're causing strife among their coworkers and that it was a mistake to hire them. Fortunately, if you run your company and your hiring process well, this situation is rare.

Don't pull a bait-and-switch either. If, as in our hyperbolic example, an employee tells you they don't like the flavor of the coffee, don't reply, "Don't worry about it." You asked for open lines of communication, so now you need to listen; otherwise, you'll foster resentment.

If you're not going to make a change, explain why. For example: "I totally understand you don't like the flavor of the coffee. Thank you for bringing that to my attention. We've had studies done about which coffee's the most popular across the whole organization and where we can get the best price. We've evaluated what you recommended, and it doesn't currently meet our parameters for the procurement of coffee, but thank you again for coming to me with this issue."

PILLAR #8: DETERMINE AN ACCEPTABLE TEAM MEETING CADENCE

I once worked at a company where we never had scheduled sales meetings. Never. Then, out of the blue, some higher-up would say, "I need all your information—have it ready by tomorrow." As you'd expect, people scrambled to pull together what they needed to present, and the meeting was not well-run as a result. Moreover, the whole process felt unnecessarily contentious and anxiety-provoking. This is an example of a cadence that is not frequent enough.

On the other end of the spectrum, some organizations constantly invite people to meetings. Someone sends an invite to talk about a product, for example, and everyone's supposed to show up in an hour. Then someone else has an issue around personnel, so there's another invite. Employees' work is frequently interrupted, even if they don't need to be part of any given conversation, so they aren't able to focus on the core functions of their job.

When it comes to meeting cadence, you need a predictable and reliable structure. Of course, emergency meetings will happen when there's truly a fire that can't wait, but in a well-run organization, that should be rare. Employees who are frustrated with meeting cadence are often encountering one of these two scenarios:

- Their boss demands their availability at any given moment, which is unpredictable and counterproductive.
- Their boss never meets with them, which means they have no idea if they're doing a good job or not.

Assess the number of meetings you have. Don't create meetings for meetings' sake, and double-check that all scheduled meetings are necessary. Striking the right balance will create more satisfied employees and more valuable meetings.

TIP #1: IMPLEMENT THE RULE OF SIX

I once read that a team meeting should include no more than six people because too many voices results in there not being enough time for each voice to be heard.

There are various ways to pull together effective meeting sizes based on your structure and specific needs, but meetings should generally include a leader or manager and the people they directly supervise. However, what if you have twelve people reporting to you? If that's the case, I'm going to guess that you're feeling overwhelmed—and that it's time to assign a team lead!

If you don't yet have that mid-level structure in place, then split the group in half and coordinate two meetings. Otherwise, it's unlikely that everyone will have the chance to get their points across in the allotted time, which I believe shouldn't exceed ninety minutes.

TIP #2: MAKE SURE THE RIGHT PEOPLE—AND *ONLY* THE RIGHT PEOPLE—ARE IN THE ROOM

A passionate workforce needs to execute on their work. The more meetings you ask them to attend, the less time and focus they have to allocate to their core responsibilities. As a result, they might get burned out trying to keep up or fall behind and receive a reprimand—both situations that foster resentment.

Make sure that if you're inviting someone to a meeting, they truly need to be there more than they need to be focusing on their core responsibilities. You can make their attendance optional or even invite them for part of the meeting, then allow them to leave once their contribution is complete. Often, though, your employees can receive a notification after a decision has been made rather than sit through the deliberations.

PILLAR #9: CONDUCT REGULAR ONE-ON-ONE MEETINGS

It's common for people in less optimized companies to have weekly meetings but no one-on-ones. Groups are great for solving many problems together, but it takes individual interactions to foster personal and professional alignment between managers and employees.

Personal and professional concerns often blur together

in the modern work world, so it's important for managers to regularly check in on their employees. After all, there are many issues that people won't feel comfortable discussing in front of a group, particularly if there are already several pressing agenda items that affect the whole team or company. For example, someone may be having an issue with their colleague or a challenge with their child. Give them privacy and confidentiality in regular one-on-ones so that they trust you enough to share their concerns.

How often should you have one-on-ones? You'll find that every week tends to be too much; there's just not enough to talk about. On the other hand, after more than a month, too much time has elapsed for you to foster connection. So, I recommend having one-on-ones every two to three weeks.

Remember, it takes flexibility and discernment to find the best cadence for your organization. For example, I used to hold one-on-ones every week, but over time, I found that every two weeks worked better for my team. There may even be some unique situations when it makes sense to meet more or less frequently. Whatever the case, be intentional about how often you have one-on-ones, and use your observations and reasoning to back up your decision.

My fundamental argument is that one-on-ones should be neither too frequent nor too infrequent. Beyond that, you decide what's best for you and your team.

TIP #1: MAKE ONE-ON-ONES INFORMAL

One-on-one meetings should be about thirty minutes—they don't need to be longer—and I like to have them unstructured, with no agenda.

It's always fascinating where the conversation ends up.

Sometimes an employee who is going through a really difficult time ends up in tears, but I've had other meetings where we spent the whole time talking about random animals in the Amazon. Regardless of the topics you discuss, the purpose of these meetings is to forge personal and professional connections. By keeping the approach informal, you can connect in whatever way makes the most sense for that individual.

TIP #2: ASK OPEN-ENDED QUESTIONS

In general, I let the conversation go where it will, based on the needs and situation of the person I'm meeting with. For instance, I once signed on to a call as an employee was laughing. When I asked what was up, she told me her mother was in town and had just said something funny, so I asked her about her Mother's Day. I think of these interactions as "break room talks."

When the conversation needs a jumpstart, I keep a list of open-ended questions:

- How are you?
  - "I'm good"
- Awesome, why are you doing good?
- What's bothering you that shouldn't be?
  - Don't ask "if" something is bothering them because they will say no. Assume something is bothering them.
- How can I help you?

I also have a list of the 15 Pillars in front of me so that I can touch on any that seem relevant.

SKIP-LEVEL MEETINGS

In addition to regular one-on-ones with their managers, I can't overstate how valuable it is for employees to have access to their superiors. For example, I talk to all of my employees at least once a month because I have a small company and can afford to do so. Even in larger organizations, though, people should be able to talk to their boss's boss; otherwise, they'll feel siloed, like they're just a number.

People really appreciate the opportunity to talk to a regional director, VP, or CEO, particularly if they are interested in growing into leadership roles themselves. That access boosts their enthusiasm, engagement, and passion—and adds a different flavor to their everyday interactions.

For leaders, these skip-level meetings are a great way to proactively connect with employees, rather than only hearing from them if something is going wrong. They're a way of lifting them up, of showing you respect them and think they're worth your time. They're a way to get valuable intel about what is going well and what needs improvement, and new ideas and opportunities may arise. You may even recognize a rising star who needs to be groomed for a promotion.

Regardless of the outcome, skip-level meetings make people feel important and valued, which moves them toward the passionate end of the Passionate Workforce Spectrum and keeps them there.

PILLAR #10: OFFER REWARDS AND RECOGNITION

People love rewards and recognition for a job well done. Yes, their salary is important, but a lot of the time, people are really chasing clout. They want to be recognized.

That isn't to say you can't use money as a reward, because obviously you can, and everyone appreciates that. If someone does an amazing job one quarter, you can certainly cut them a bonus check. However, when it comes to rewarding, I like to get personal: a sticker to put on their Harley, a new grill set because their old one got stolen. Personalization shows you're paying attention, seeing people's humanity, and caring.

Once, we had an employee who did a phenomenal job on a project. We found out she was planning a trip with her sisters, so we rewarded her work by picking up the cost of the Airbnb she was staying at. Obviously, this employee loved that she was getting something valuable for free, but she also loved the clout she earned within her family for being recognized by her company.

People want that clout within a company too: pats on their back, congratulations, a little bit of spotlight. Fortunately, there are many natural opportunities to recognize employees. For example, I often celebrate workplace anniversaries over our Slack channel so that everyone has the opportunity to acknowledge an employee's time with and impact on the company. (I don't present rewards publicly because they're often financial and can potentially stoke tension or jealousy. They're not secret, but they're not announced.)

To keep an ongoing emphasis on positivity and passion, consider recognition before rewards. Recognizing people offers a great ROI, stoking passion without requiring you to dig into your budget. Reserve rewards for truly exceptional performance.

TIP #1: RECOGNIZE/REWARD RANDOMLY AND EMOTIONALLY

What do I mean by "randomly and emotionally"? Let's start with what I *don't* mean. I don't mean Christmas bonuses.

A Christmas bonus is no longer a reward or a recognition; it's an expectation. When you've created an expectation, you can only go down—you can never go up. The way I operate, and the way I would encourage others to operate, is with the understanding that anything you give to employees can never be taken away. They become expectations to employees, and if and when they are taken away, you can be sure that there will be a visible decrease in passion.

With that framework in mind, an example of a random reward is when we called an employee in the middle of our quarterly meeting to tell him we were sending him a check for $5,000 because of his exceptional performance. It was random, not anything that he could expect to happen again.

An example of an emotional reward is covering the hardworking employee's Airbnb. We recognized what was important to her and gave her a reward that aligned with her priority of spending time with the people she loves.

Random and emotional also means recognition and rewards have to come from the heart, not from a quota, a blanket rule, or a rigid schedule. If they're overly structured, people can see through your intentions, and what you give loses its meaning. When you give a reward, go for something that will make the recipient feel excited, like finding a $20 bill in their back pocket.

So, don't reward in equal measure across your employees because not all employees are doing equal levels of work. You're shooting yourself in the foot if you treat everyone like they're excelling, regardless of performance, because when everyone gets a reward, effectively no one gets one. When everyone knows rewards will go out like clockwork, unrelated to exceptional contributions, they come to expect them and devalue them

On the other hand, when rewards and recognition mean something, it doesn't matter how long ago you last rewarded a person. The dose of dopamine hits them just as hard. Plus, they'll remember that they got rewarded *because* they worked their butt off.

TIP #2: DON'T REWARD OUT OF GUILT

Rewarding out of guilt often looks like giving everyone an award. For example, if I wanted to recognize five people because they earned it but I was worried about the others feeling bad, I might make up a lame reason to award them anyway, even though they didn't earn it. Don't do that.

My approach stems from my Pentecostal faith, which is that *God loves a cheerful giver.* This phrase brought me great clarity, so now if I see someone on the street, I don't give them money to avoid others thinking I'm a jerk; I give because my heart and the Holy Spirit call me to do so.

Not only are giving out of guilt or fear of looking bad selfish ways of giving, but also, the more you're worried about how people perceive you, the more that worry distorts your behavior. If you really want to be an altruistic and noble leader or manager, give out of the purity of your heart. Only give because your heart tells you to recognize another person's efforts.

So many companies have mission statements and social initiatives that have nothing to do with their ethics and everything to do with PR. It's all a facade. Everyone knows they're making empty promises to chase trends. In contrast, lead in alignment with your morals, starting with giving cheerfully rather than guiltily.

TIP #3: PRAISE IN PUBLIC AND CRITICIZE IN PRIVATE

If an employee just completed a big project, send out a blast as wide as you can—to the extent it's appropriate—and be as specific as possible. After all, it's not particularly meaningful to say, "Ryan did great this quarter." Get into the details about what he did and why it was exceptional.

On the other hand, if Ryan just dropped the ball on a project, deal with it one-on-one or within a small circle, as appropriate. Doing otherwise will only fuel the gossip mill and create resentment toward and within Ryan.

PILLAR #11: ASSESS EMPLOYEES' JOB SATISFACTION

Ensuring that a person is aligned with a job should begin with the interview process. Think: GWC. Do they *get* it? Do they *want* it? Do they have the *capacity* to do it? When you bring people in correctly and with intention, then you can start strong. It takes less effort to keep people passionate than to convert them to passion.

However, even a person who is perfectly aligned with their job to begin with may experience a shift over time as they—and the business—grow. Tasks they used to enjoy years ago might not be so exciting anymore, or their responsibilities may have changed in a way that doesn't align with their skills and interests. This is a natural evolution that you need to account for.

How do you account for loss of passion over time? You have to continually provide reasons and opportunities for your employees to be passionate through an ongoing and open dialogue.

One-on-ones are a great way to monitor how people are feeling about their job and whether anything is bothering them. If their goals have changed, for instance, then you need to work with that. Nothing stays static forever.

When people aren't happy about their job, there are three things you can do:

1. Remedy the issue
2. Explain why the situation can't change and have them accept that answer
3. Have them leave the organization

If someone wants to travel all the time and you don't offer that option, they don't belong in your company. If someone wants to be fully remote and that's not an opportunity, they don't belong there. On the other hand, if someone's passion has shifted toward a different set of responsibilities that are necessary and bring value to your company, then you can help them transition into the new right seat. Or, if they would be passionate about their role if they had the right tools and different support, then you can remedy that situation too.

An essential key to effective leadership is getting people to trust you enough to tell you when something is bothering them. If they avoid speaking up, their frustration will fester, leading to resentment and ultimately accepting calls from recruiters. By then, they're likely beyond saving, so nip the problems in the bud by continually checking whether they like their job.

TIP #1: DELEGATE AND ELEVATE RESPONSIBILITIES

To delegate and elevate responsibilities, divide a sheet into four quadrants:

- Top Left: What work do you love to do that you're great at?
- Top Right: What work do you like to do that you're good at?
- Bottom Left: What work do you not like to do that you're good at?
- Bottom Right: What work do you not like to do that you're not good at?

DELEGATE AND ELEVATE

LOVE/GREAT	LIKE/GOOD

DON'T LIKE/GOOD	DON'T LIKE/NOT GOOD

Have employees write each of their responsibilities in one of the quadrants, and then discuss the quadrants during your one-on-ones. That way, you'll be able to get a clearer picture of which tasks actually cause them frustration and which ones they just need time to grow in.

To play to people's strengths and passions, you will want to remove responsibilities that fall into their bottom right box. Where it makes sense, you may also want to adjust some of the other boxes. You can't please everyone, but whether you remove a task they don't like or add a task that they do, you should be able to give them something that edges them toward passion.

PILLAR #12: CULTIVATE STRONG, RESILIENT RELATIONSHIPS

Historically, leaders and managers have been advised not to hire people they like, but I wholeheartedly disagree. I actively hire people I like because I, like most people, often spend more time at work than at home. If I'm hiring somebody who does a good job, but he's a schmuck, what does that do to my overall quality of life?

We need to enjoy the people we work with. As a leader or manager, you need to make sure you bring in people whose personalities blend in well with the rest of the team. Fortunately, there are a lot of different personalities that can blend well together.

TIP #1: FOLLOW THE CORE VALUES OF THE ORGANIZATION

When people share core values, you can expect them to get along with each other, so use the core values of your organization to hire, fire, and promote. Just one person who's not on the same page as everyone else can throw the entire team off; a single negative, arrogant, or rude team member can wreak a lot of havoc within their department.

In contrast, adding employees who get along with your workforce doesn't dilute your corporate culture. Instead, it creates an echo chamber, increasing everyone's power.

TIP #2: UNDERSTAND THAT CONFLICT IS HEALTHY

Even when you hire, fire, and promote according to your organization's core values, conflicts will occur. That's normal, even healthy, in an environment focused on growth. But when there is conflict, colleagues who are part of a passionate workforce have the capacity to resolve issues amongst themselves.

Let's say Rebecca works with Tyler, who shows up late multiple times. In a passionate workforce, Rebecca can respectfully and candidly explain, "Tyler, I know you're super busy. I feel you. You're showing up late a lot, and it's causing me a lot of frustration. I would really appreciate it if you could make a conscious effort to arrive on time." Tyler can then take her feedback to heart and work to resolve the issue at hand.

Not every interaction will happen perfectly, but when you hire based on core values, you should rarely have to mediate between parties.

PILLAR #13: ENSURE EMPLOYEES FEEL A SENSE OF PURPOSE

There's a story that President John F. Kennedy went up to a NASA janitor and asked, "What do you do?"

His janitor answered, "I'm helping get a man on the moon."

Maybe this story is a bit of an exaggeration, but it's still fair enough. If you helped President John F. Kennedy, you helped get a man on the moon.

A common frustration you hear nowadays is "I'm just a cog in the wheel. I'm just a number." When someone feels that way, that automatically reduces the amount of passion.

So, it's up to leaders and managers to make sure they're showing people how they're making a contribution to the company, no matter what position they are in. The impact looks different for each person, but it all adds up.

TIP #1: CLIENT SPOTLIGHT IMPACT

Employees don't care about the company hitting revenue numbers. Executives do. When an employee wonders, *Am I making a difference in the company?* they're really wondering, *What are the emotions I'm creating through my work? How is my effort improving other people's quality of life?*

Whether it's their coworkers, clients, vendors, or the community, employees want to have a positive impact on people, so it's your responsibility to make sure that everybody understands the difference they're making. For example, every quarter you can invite your clients to interview with the company. If they agree, spend the first half of the interview asking about their responsibilities and interests; during the second half, ask about how your employees' actions enhanced their quality of life.

The client might say something like, "I really needed this project done, and it was done right on time." Then the employee might think to themselves, "*Oh, that was me!*" Or the client might say, "We had this really tough hurdle to overcome, and you guys came through." And then maybe one team thinks, "*Oh, that was us!*"

TIP #2: REMIND YOURSELF TO REWARD AND RECOGNIZE PEOPLE

Remember when I talked about setting a reminder every Friday to reward or recognize people that week? You don't have to reward or recognize someone every week—people will see through your intentions if you force it—but do take time to reflect. Did anyone do anything that warrants a shout out?

This could be as simple as pulling the janitor aside and saying, "Hey, you do a great job keeping this place clean. Thank you." Or maybe sending a blast over the company Slack channel to give someone credit for a great sale.

PILLAR #14: COMPENSATE THE WORKFORCE APPROPRIATELY

This pillar is a little bit more black and white than the others. A person is either compensated appropriately or they're not.

Money matters. People being compensated appropriately matters. Beth's not going to be happy if she thinks she's worth more than she's being paid. If someone feels they're not being compensated appropriately, they are likely either actively trying to find another job or are thinking about finding another job.

TIP #1: DON'T NEGOTIATE

When an employee approaches you for a salary increase, listen to their justification, then give them a yes or a no—and let them know ahead of time that those are the only two possible outcomes of salary discussions. Do not meet them in the middle.

Let's say you are approached for a 10 percent raise, and you counter with 5 percent. Do you think that employee will be happy with that 5 percent raise? Nope. They're thinking about how you value them at half of what they value themselves. And you still gave them the 5 percent, so you just paid more money to piss them off.

When employees know you're not going to negotiate, they think really hard about what they're going to ask for. If the amount they propose is still not financially viable for your company, say no, knowing that they will probably leave.

There's an acronym I learned in business school called BATNA: Best Alternative to a Negotiated Agreement. It's a fancy way of saying, "What's your line in the sand?" How valuable is this employee to you? I've personally given people huge raises, and I've also denied very minimal requests. The most consistent thing about me is that I treat everybody differently, based on their performance and value to the organization.

Ultimately, it's a win-win. Either someone gets the raise they ask for and they're ecstatic, or you say no and they leave.

Let's say you don't have complete authority over who gets how much. If one of your best guys comes in and asks for a raise, and the higher-ups deny the request, use respectful candor. Say, "I don't have the authority to do that. I think you're worth it, but I have to go and speak to the powers that be. I'm going to give it my all, and I'll come back and tell you what I'm able to do, and then you can tell me how you feel about it."

Regardless of whether you give an employee a raise or not, if they're living to work and not working to live, their job satisfaction will not be high. The person who dies with the most money doesn't win.

PILLAR #15: ACHIEVE A GOOD WORK-LIFE BLEND

A work–life blend is different from work–life balance. When you have work–life balance, there's a separation between your professional work and your personal life.

For example, at my first job, we had email, but only used it very rarely. We did everything on paper. This meant that I couldn't do my job until I was in the office, and I couldn't do anything after I left the office. There was an obvious split between work time and personal time.

With today's technology (e.g., cell phones, email, and other technologies), there doesn't have to be a hard line between the two. When you have a work–life blend, you engage with work in your personal life, and you engage with your personal life at work.

This isn't something just for leaders and managers. We've all seen CEOs leave to go golfing or show up late with no consequences, but it's hypocritical and dehumanizing when other employees are not afforded the same flexibility. Are we really going to give people "the look" because the only dentist appointment they could get is at 2:00 p.m.? It's incredibly demoralizing when you get judged for just being a human in the workplace.

Your employees need to feel like they're on a par with you when it comes to making the best choices for their own lives. So, allow people to take lunch for an hour or two if they choose. Let them pick up their kids. If they've got a migraine, make space for them to step away. These are all normal, human experiences.

If you don't think your employees are already doing these things, let me tell you, they're doing them. You might as well allow them, within reason. Just encourage them to let their teams know what's going on.

TIP #1: ENCOURAGE COMMUNICATION

Communication is an important part of achieving a good work–life blend. Let's say Becky wants to leave for a two-hour lunch. In a passionate workforce, she respectfully communicates that to her team, and her team can plan around her absence. They can work on another project that doesn't need her oversight or input. They can move forward and function in Becky's absence, and she feels humanized, appreciated, empowered, and respected as a result.

Now, if someone needs Becky there, they need to respectfully and candidly communicate, "I hear you, Becky. We have a client coming to visit in an hour, and they want to meet with you." Becky, being passionate, might say, "Ah, you're right. It slipped my mind. Thanks, I'll take my break later."

Ultimately, you've just got to be humanistic about the process. A long lunch doesn't supersede meeting with a client, but if Becky's son was in a car accident, that is a different story. With each situation, you have to weigh and balance priorities.

As a leader or manager, you need to track things like this to make sure they aren't being abused. Take note of when employees are taking time off or leaving early, but more importantly, measure whether or not they're getting their work done.

TAKE STOCK

The 15 Pillars are a great way for you to take stock of the passion of your workforce, which is the lifeblood of your organization, and to identify any shortcomings in your leadership and management ability. To that end, it's great to have everyone on a team or in the organization as a whole reflect on the pillars through an anonymous survey, allowing an overarching, systemic view of where the group is excelling and where it's falling behind.

Thinking back to my stint forklift racing, I realize that Mr. Dube:

- Provided us with the necessary tools
- Empowered us to make our own decision (to a fault)
- Assigned tasks reasonable for our bandwidth
- Treated us with respectful candor (but only for the one brief interaction we had)
- Compensated us appropriately, given that we were high schoolers making minimum wage
- Allowed for good work–life blend, except that it was all life and no work

However, he did not:

- Give us clear direction or expectations
- Instill an understanding of the greater purpose of our work and the company (if, for example, he'd explained that the warehouse stored drugs to save cancer patients, we probably would have felt more motivated)
- Have an acceptable meeting cadence (he disappeared!)
- Reward or recognize us (he wasn't around, and as a result, we didn't do anything worth rewarding)
- Foster a sense of enjoyment of our job
- Set up a situation in which we could enjoy our coworkers
- Help us feel like we were making a difference in the company

In the absence of knowledge about how we were experiencing the job, and lacking sufficient leadership and management skills, he paid us to do nothing, let us go, and then had to start from scratch with vacant positions.

I did an anonymous survey of the 15 Pillars with my employees, and I scored above nine on all of them except one; regarding appropriate compensation, The FDA Group scored 8.86. Those are fantastic results, but does that mean I should rest on my laurels? Absolutely not. It was just a snapshot in time that told me we were on the right track. Passion takes investment and maintenance, so I am always looking for ways to improve and grow; otherwise, we'll backslide.

Depending on the size of your organization, it might make sense to survey everyone or to survey a more targeted group, such as your direct reports and one or two layers down, capturing the individuals you have influence over, directly or indirectly. The CEO of GE, for instance, probably doesn't want to survey the healthcare and lighting divisions or the Mexico and Philippines operations together because each of those groups have different needs and structures. The information gained in the aggregate would be too broad. It would be like surveying the entire planet on how POTUS is doing; the aggregate answer isn't very useful for driving domestic policy.

However, when you decide to assess your employees' sense of how the organization measures up against the pillars, dig deep into the answers, take the importance of these principles to heart, and use them to keep leveling up.

Of course, this strategy is predicated on the assumption that you care about your workforce—or, at least, that you care about them sticking around. So, it's time to ask yourself, *What type of leader/manager am I?*

CHAPTER 6

WHAT TYPE OF LEADER/ MANAGER ARE YOU?

"Great leaders live in a constant state of being comfortably uncomfortable."

—NICK CAPMAN

Over the course of this book, we've explored why a passionate workforce matters to a business, how to create a cultural framework that encourages that passion, and what you can do to spark and sustain it in new hires and long-term employees. However, there's an important piece of the puzzle we haven't yet addressed: you.

As a leader of a team or a company, it's just as important to assess yourself as it is to assess your employees. This is especially true if you're struggling to generate passion in your workforce—even with the helpful tips provided in previous chapters. Completing your self-assessment will allow you to better understand the type of leader you currently are, confront insufficiencies, and set a course for improvement.

TAKE THE LEADERSHIP & MANAGEMENT ASSESSMENT

Once again, we can turn to the 15 Pillars to understand where we succeed as leaders and where we fall short. Give yourself a score from zero to ten on each pillar, then average all of your scores.

As a reminder, these are the 15 Pillars:

- Pillar #1: Give Clear Direction
- Pillar #2: Provide the Necessary Tools to Complete the Job
- Pillar #3: Empower Employees to Make Decisions on Their Own
- Pillar #4: Operate with the Greater Good in Mind
- Pillar #5: Respect Employees' Bandwidth
- Pillar #6: Set Clear Expectations
- Pillar #7: Communicate Respectfully and Candidly
- Pillar #8: Determine an Acceptable Team Meeting Cadence
- Pillar #9: Conduct Regular One-on-One Meetings
- Pillar #10: Offer Rewards and Recognition
- Pillar #11: Assess Employees' Job Satisfaction
- Pillar #12: Cultivate Strong, Resilient Relationships
- Pillar #13: Ensure Employees Feel a Sense of Purpose
- Pillar #14: Compensate the Workforce Appropriately
- Pillar #15: Achieve a Good Work-Life Blend

Your overall average will tell you if you're a **Toxic Leader** (0–6), an **Adequate Leader** (7–8), or a **Champion Leader** (9–10).

If you made it this far in the book, you won't score zero or one, at the very least. Congratulations!

However, be really honest with yourself. Give yourself

all tens if you believe you deserve them, but consider: would your employees give you all tens, too? Ask them to complete the same assessment for you and find out.

This second part is the most important. All employees who are asked to participate will grade their boss in each of the 15 Pillars, and an average will be taken.

You need to challenge your core beliefs and be as objective as possible. If you give yourself all tens and see that your employees gave you all fives, one of two things will happen: either you will think, *My employees are all crazy*, or you will have an "Aha!" moment. The road to becoming a great leader starts with having that "Aha!" moment.

Once you have your average score, locate yourself along the Leadership & Management Spectrum. From there, consider how to move yourself closer to where you want to be.

LEADERSHIP & MANAGEMENT ASSESSMENT

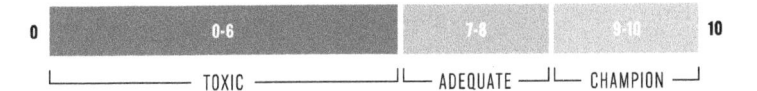

```
0        0-6              7-8        9-10      10
└────── TOXIC ──────┴── ADEQUATE ──┴── CHAMPION ─┘
```

TOXIC LEADERS (0-6)

I once had a client who dressed like a mafia boss: white Italian shirt, buttons undone, chest hair out, gold chain around his neck, True Religion jeans, and fancy chino shoes. Of course, he rode to work in a Lamborghini, and whenever he arrived at work, blustering through the office like a tornado, the vibe of the place would instantly change. *Oh no, here he comes.*

This client would down eight shots of espresso and randomly interrupt meetings. He'd demand to be briefed on a project he wasn't at all involved with. He would either give no direction or horrible direction. He wouldn't give his overworked employees the resources they needed to do their job. A rumor even surfaced that he was having an extramarital affair with one of his employees. I could go on.

There's nothing wrong with Italian shirts and gold chains and fancy cars, but you have to remember that you're constantly creating a story of yourself through your words and actions. And your employees are reading that story. There's no place in this day and age for toxic leaders who swing their power around like a child holding a hammer.

Toxic leaders:

- Have no predictability or accountability
- Are a disruptive presence in the workplace
- Nitpick and micromanage their employees
- Don't provide the tools or support that employees need to succeed
- Don't reward or recognize employees

At their worst, toxic leaders will:

- Actively harm the organization
- Exploit employees
- Lie, manipulate, or humiliate colleagues

Toxic leaders don't care about people. They care about money. They care about profit. Then they turn around and ask, "Why don't my employees care about me and my company?"

Because you didn't give them a reason to care.

ADEQUATE LEADERS (7–8)

Adequate leaders generally wear a suit, maybe glasses, are well groomed, and drive a modest vehicle like an Acura TL. They may be moderately wealthy, but they don't flaunt it. In fact, you probably don't see them much at all; they tend to stick to their office rather than mingle with their employees.

Earlier in my career, I gave a presentation to forty people. Beforehand, I had no real emotional or technical support from my boss. During the presentation, he sat in the audience with his arms crossed, scowling in a way that made me feel judged. He gave me no nods, no wide eyes.

We were trying to win a client, but that presentation felt like an evaluation. I could sense the hierarchy between our respective positions.

Adequate leaders:

- Don't cause chaos in the workplace
- Are oblivious to the deeper reasons behind employees' actions and/or words
- Don't exhibit curiosity about how they can improve
- Don't afford employees the same flexibility they afford themselves
- Cling to an old-school leadership style: *Why should I congratulate or reward you for a job well done? I expect you to do your job well.*

In general, my old boss wasn't a jerk. He didn't cause much anxiety or disruption, but he also had no qualms about making his superiority and expectations known. He had a you-do-for-me mindset, so even though I could ask questions, I couldn't expect support. In short, his appearance and demeanor were adequate—not toxic, but not great either.

CHAMPION LEADERS (9–10)

I had another boss named Shane who had such great energy that I felt special from the very first interview. He looked like an offensive lineman for a football team but, like the adequate leader, was clean shaven and suited up. Interestingly, he was more relaxed, often sporting a five o'clock shadow or a loosened tie by Friday.

When I was hired, I noticed that he never stayed in his office for long; he was always looking around. He took a hands-on approach in my training, and even after I had ramped up, he always removed all distractions to listen to my problems, despite how busy he was.

Champion leaders:

- Implement a work–life blend in the workplace
- Guide the company toward their vision
- Communicate in a respectfully candid manner
- Are ethical and capable, as well as empathetic and personable
- Demonstrate a hunger for knowledge
- Are always looking to grow

It's important to note that the support I received from that great boss wasn't exclusive to me. He would take employees out to lunch, actively listen when he asked about their personal lives, and give practical advice about advancing their careers. He never failed to provide a shoulder to lean on in the face of failure or a celebratory high-five in the glow of success. He was clearly invested in his people, never critical except when feedback would help you grow.

That's how you become a champion leader.

BECOME A CHAMPION LEADER

A toxic or adequate leader cannot cultivate a truly passionate workforce—only a champion leader can. At the same time, a passionate workforce enables a boss to be a champion leader.

Think of it like a stand-up show. The leader is the comedian on stage, and the employees are the audience. A comedian can be hilarious, but with a bad audience, he'll tank. Similarly, he can have a really great crowd who wants him to succeed, but if he bombs on stage, then the crowd will politely clap at best.

What you want is to be Bill Burr at Radio City Music Hall. You're killing it on stage, and the audience is eating it up. You have the skills and knowledge to be a comedic expert, and your audience is giving you the energy and support you need to make them laugh.

To become a champion leader, you must first get comfortable being uncomfortable. You need to be aware that you don't know what you don't know. Fortunately, if you're reading this book, it's probably because you're curious. You're hungry for knowledge. You want to discover the next incremental thing you can do better than other leaders. So, be selfish about your hunger for knowledge.

As a leader or manager, the onus is on you to keep your company moving forward. If you're not moving forward, you're moving backward. If you're not getting better, you're getting worse. Nobody stays still, so always be evolving.

Let that evolution start with the 15 Pillars. Identify the places where there is room for improvement—and embrace that prospect. Lean in to what you can do better, and let passion be the driving force for everything you do in your business.

I started by pretending to care about my employees, and

then a funny thing happened...I actually started to care about them. That simple act led me on an incredible journey that has brought me to you.

You're already on a path to becoming a champion leader—where else will your journey take you?

CONCLUSION

You've now learned many practical tips for cultivating a passionate workforce, but the work goes much deeper than that. It goes back to the center of the onion: ethical and moral happiness. You have the tools to improve other people's quality of life—and your own—so think about what you're going to accomplish.

No, really think about it. If you cultivate a passionate workforce, they'll love their job. That means they won't go home stressed, ready to complain to their family. Instead, they'll go home happy, which means they'll have the energy to give their family loving attention. They'll have a sense of pride and ownership when they go to parties and talk about what they do for work. They'll be able to buy that second home or finally go on that vacation. They'll get to develop these strong lifelong bonds with their coworkers—bonds that will continue even past when they leave the company.

Through the simple action of reading this book and learning from it, you've started a domino effect. First, you'll improve your life. Then, you'll improve your employees' lives.

Then, they'll improve their partners' lives, their children' lives, and their relationships with friends and coworkers. You'll send a shockwave of positivity throughout different levels of your community.

Like I said, if you only take one thing away, let it be this: implement the 15 Pillars in your workplace. Use them, measure them, and improve upon them.

If you think anyone you love and care about could benefit from reading this book, then tell them to read it. Pay it forward. Pass the torch. Help someone else take advantage of what you're taking advantage of. At the end of the day, we're all trying to reach the highest level of Maslow's pyramid, self-actualization.

Everything you do should come back to love—for your family, friends, colleagues, and fellow man. So, do one last thing for me: before you go to bed tonight, call someone up and tell them you love them. Give your spouse a hug. Tell your kids how proud you are of them. Then take that same love and apply it to running your business.

A passionate workforce comes down to its people. And people need that love.

ACKNOWLEDGMENTS

I would like to thank my Lord and Savior Jesus Christ for His saving grace and mercy, as well as thank the Holy Spirit for dwelling inside me and guiding me to be righteous in this fleeting life.

I would like to thank my wife, who is the purest version of what a wife and mother should be. I only wish more people could come to know you and learn from you.

I would like to thank my two children, Vinicius and Melyssa. Your morality, integrity, and drive to be the best that you can be make me so proud. You fill my heart with overwhelming love and admiration.

I would like to thank my American family members, including and not limited to my late father, who is my hero, my brother Blake, my uncle Donald, my aunt Bonnie, my late grandmother Winnie, my late great-aunt Velma, and everyone else I've had the pleasure and privilege of sitting at a dinner table with.

I would like to thank my Brazilian family members, including and not limited to my nephews Marquito and

Lukas, my mother-in-law Valmira, my aunt-in-law Valdeci and her husband Elveso, my sister-in-law Edvania, my Goddaughter Anna-Laura, all of my nieces, and everyone else in Belo Horizonte and Gurupi whom I've had the pleasure and privilege of having a churrasco with.

I would like to thank my friends, including and not limited to Nick, Adam, Seth, Inky, Kevin, Marc, Tom, Markie, Spike, Sabino, and everyone else I've had the pleasure of sharing tears and beers with.

I would like to thank those individuals I've had the benefit of knowing through Vistage. Your professional insights and friendships have most certainly allowed me to continue to grow and improve.

I would like to thank my employees for their professionalism and friendship. You are the greatest inspiration for me writing this book.

Finally, I would like to thank the team at Scribe for everything they did to make this the best book it could be.

ABOUT THE AUTHOR

NICHOLAS CAPMAN is the CEO of The FDA Group, a life science consulting firm. In addition to assisting some of the largest and most recognized life science companies, Nicholas and his firm have contributed to many media outlets on the topic of FDA regulations, such as Fox Business, Bloomberg, CNN, MSNBC, *The New York Times*, and the Associated Press. The FDA Group is a two-time *Boston Business Journal* Fast 50 recipient and has been included on the Inc. 5000 list four years in a row under Nicholas' leadership. In addition, The FDA Group has consistently achieved an A+ rating with the Better Business Bureau, been certified as a Great Place to Work, and as of the publishing of this book, has touted a 4.8 out of 5.0 star rating on Glassdoor.com, proving the effectiveness of his methodology. Nicholas received his Bachelors of Arts and Master of Business Administration Degrees from the University of Massachusetts Amherst. In order to mentor younger generations of business leaders, he has been a judge for several years for both the Massachusetts State Science & Engineering Fair as well as the Network for Teaching Entrepreneurship.

Milton Keynes UK
Ingram Content Group UK Ltd.
UKHW020317070624
443692UK00011B/203/J